TIME

FULL STOP
OR
QUESTION
MARK

?

STEPHEN BISHOP

 Zaccmedia

Published by Zaccmedia
www.zaccmedia.com
info@zaccmedia.com

Published May 2017

ISBN: 978-1-911211-61-7

British Library Cataloguing-in-Publication Data
A catalogue record for this book is available from the British Library.

CONTENTS

INTRODUCTION

They now appear somewhat faded and worn. But that's not surprising since they were painted onto the pavement surfaces well over a decade ago. Since that time many footsteps have passed over those yellow, car-tyre sized circles, with a line across them marking the track of the Greenwich Meridian. This part of London, near the starting point of that line but heavily populated, was not necessarily the ideal place to paint them!

However, it seemed a good idea to commemorate the year AD 2000 with a reminder in this way that east London was bisected by this invisible but important meridian. Other places, of greater fame, possibly instituted more worthy (and expensive) markers. But very few (if any) could claim that this invisible line ran the entire length of their borough.

MEASURING TIME

Of course the Greenwich Meridian is in one sense an entirely arbitrary line. It may be seen as a quirk of history. London was once a particularly powerful and influential city. That was when it was selected as the internationally recognised location for zero degrees longitude. The decision to do so was made at the 1884 International Meridian Conference held in Washington DC, ending a rivalry in which other nations had instituted their own 'Meridians'.

The Greenwich Meridian doesn't, of itself, measure time. It's simply the means by which time can be uniformly calibrated. The word 'meridian' is derived from the Latin word *merides*, which means 'midday'. Use of the abbreviations 'a.m.' and 'p.m.' (meaning, respectively, 'ante-meridian' and 'post-meridian') enables a time either before or after noon in the 12-hour clock to be distinguished.

LOST DAYS

But there are problems! Scientists have established that the earth's rotation is not constant. Data show that it is slowing down. This means that our incredibly accurate atomic clocks are not quite so precise. Again this points to what may be considered the arbitrary way in which we measure 'time'. Perhaps the most extreme example of the practical relevance of this aspect of life arose in 1752. That was the year when the English Parliament passed an Act decreeing that the country change from using the Julian calendar to the Gregorian one. The former had failed to take into account the fact that leap years weren't applicable every four years as had been instituted since Roman times. The turning of the century should not (generally) have been taken as such a year since the earth's rotation around the sun was not quite the 365 days-and-a bit that was thought. So from 1582 (when the Gregorian system was first instigated by Pope Gregory XIII) countries were progressively amending their calendars to address this discrepancy. For England perhaps it was a case of 'better late than never'! Eventually, introducing the new Gregorian one meant that 11 days in September 1752 were 'lost' to make the necessary adjustment. Some history books have described unrest by the general population on account of this change, people demanding that they be given back their 'missing' days!

TIME TRAVELLING

These examples all indicate the practical relevance but sometimes conflicting arbitrariness of 'time'. Humankind may be able to channel or control certain elements of nature but of time itself there is no control. We even struggle to record it accurately. Looking at it on a personal basis, we each have the same 24 hours in the day. Time cannot be bought, stored up or swapped. For some people time may 'fly' while for others it may 'drag'. Time has to be used as it comes, with no power enabling us to simulate the activity of the BBC television character Dr Who. His time-travelling exploits – having the ability to go back (and forward) in time and space – will remain as science fiction. We cannot rectify what has happened in the past, nor go into the future to determine the outcome of potential decisions in the present.

Is this the end of the matter? Is humankind forever locked in the grip of time with our 'days' being 'numbered'? In answer to those questions there is another perspective. Christians believe that God not only exists but that He speaks to us through the Bible. The latter has much to say about time and how God has intervened in this world and the lives of people on specific occasions. It also states that this activity of God is not restricted to events that took place centuries ago but is something that He undertakes in these days and in ourselves.

A FULL STOP...

One of the declarations made about God in terms of time and His interaction with people is recorded in the Old Testament. The 'Teacher' wrote: 'He [God] has made everything beautiful in its time. He has also set eternity in the human heart; yet no one can fathom what God has done from beginning to the end' (Ecclesiastes 3:11). This verse brings reassurance that God is aware of both 'time' and 'eternity'. It also underlines the fact that He is at work in both dimensions... though we would seriously struggle with how that can be achieved.

However, what we probably don't doubt is our experience of time as being a significant 'full stop'. This is not only because the passing of time marks our age and decay until death takes place. It is also because it exists as a factor of life that's completely outside of our control. Time is non-negotiable. We can measure it, record events that take place at any particular point, and project ahead to the anticipated seasons of nature and astronomical movements. But we can only operate within the inevitable progress of time, being unable to step aside from its power. It's a 'full stop' beyond which we cannot exist. The prophet Isaiah depicted the contrast between our finite passage on earth and God's eternal nature:

> All people are like grass,
>   and all their faithfulness is like the flowers
>   of the field.
> The grass withers and the flowers fall,
>   because the breath of the LORD blows on
>   them ...

The grass withers and the flowers fall,
but the word of our God endures for ever.
(Isaiah 40:6–8)

...OR A QUESTION MARK?

But that verse in Ecclesiastes 3 pointed to something else: 'He has set eternity in the human heart...' It's as though time is also being presented as a 'question mark'. The preceding words revealed the stark reality of our life, having to work hard in order to exist: 'What do workers gain from their toil? I have seen the burden God has laid on the human race' (Ecclesiastes 3:9). God then pointed out that life was more than toil and everything associated with it. We are being directed to something beyond ourselves, outside of our understanding but somehow very real. Eternity is part of that 'question mark', presenting an awesome and unimaginable perspective! We ourselves may be controlled by time but God is not. Instead, He has power over time.

So this material explores some of the implications of God's control over time and seasons described in the Bible. The following chapters will look at time in a very practical sense, Section One covering general aspects, with Section Two focusing on 'time-specific' events listed in Ecclesiastes 3.

PEOPLE

Essentially we will be looking at people in whose lives God intervened... and still does! In the same way that time affects everyone, so God wants, in some way, to impact each of us. Time is very relevant to having a growing relationship with God. So that 'question mark' will be seen as a launch pad in getting closer to Him and understanding His perspective. He operates in an eternal dimension outside of our limited conception, but He also works in our clock-focused circumstances!

FOR REFLECTION

1. What factors can make us particularly conscious of time?
2. Why does today's society focus so much on time?
3. In what ways can nature help us glimpse something of life outside of time?
4. What is reassuring in knowing that God understands our time-dominated lives?

SECTION ONE

1

WHAT'S
THE TIME?

And God said, 'Let there be lights in the vault of the sky to separate the
day from the night, and let them serve as signs to mark sacred times,
and days and years ...'
(Genesis 1:14)

The question that heads up this chapter is one that we may often ask, subconsciously if not aloud. Knowing the time is a vital part of life, even in the most mundane of activities. Catching a train, meeting for coffee, avoiding the 'school run' traffic, a dental appointment – all necessitate an awareness of time.

But what, if any, is the relevance of time when considering our relationship and walk with God? Indeed, is God aware of the constraints of time which we have to factor in? Does God's miraculous and intervening power touch upon or extend to this dimension in our lives? Our starting point in looking at these issues is to see that time is actually a vital and ongoing part of our spiritual life.

TECHNOLOGY AND TIME
Until the technologies introduced by the Industrial Revolution of the eighteenth and nineteenth centuries 'kicked in', the economy

of Great Britain was largely agricultural. Working on the land to produce crops and raise livestock did not demand precise timekeeping. Even the basic industrial processes that had been developing over many decades were not dependent upon accuracy in this area. There was an exception to this in terms of navigation on the high seas. But that apart, sunrise and sunset, together with the seasons of the year, were the main considerations. Small communities in the countryside simply focused on supplying produce and raw materials to the growing urban population. However, the latter was also becoming a force in the economy on account of manufacturing output.

When industrialisation 'moved up a gear', an unforeseen and subtle problem appeared. Transportation of goods and materials had previously been restricted to canals, coastal shipping, horse and cart, with the occasional stagecoach. Journey times were therefore measured in days and even weeks. But the new technologies now coming 'on stream' included steam locomotives and railways. These were transporting not only produce, but also people – many of them. The attraction was not only in being able to travel much longer distances via the network that was now touching many parts of the kingdom. It also meant journey times were compacted into hours and minutes.

'LOCAL TIME'

Until the advent of the new railways, the towns and cities of Great Britain kept their own time zones based on their observations of the sun. 'Local time' meant exactly that! However, this patchwork of different timings could not facilitate the uniform schedules by which passenger-carrying trains needed to operate. Indeed the railway companies of the Victorian age with routes linked to the

West Country had a particular problem. The time differences between locations could be substantial. For instance, the 'time' in Plymouth was possibly 20 minutes 'behind' that of London.

Standardisation of time for the rail network throughout the country was therefore essential in order to timetable accurate connections, arrivals and departures. The railway companies were able to institute a 'standard' time based on that derived from the Greenwich Royal Observatory within their own sphere of operations. This was by means of another new technology, the electric telegraph, enabling the 'proper' time to be broadcast throughout their system. The railways also worked hard at influencing the population in general to adhere to standard time. The designs of many railway stations, particularly at major termini and towns, featured dominant clock towers. But despite this action petty politics persisted and change was not made everywhere. It took parliamentary action by way of the 1880 Time Act to impose 'Greenwich' time throughout the country.

A CHANGED LIFESTYLE

This description of a change of over a century ago may seem obvious and very practical. But it is also relevant in a spiritual sense by way of being a 'parable'. The teaching of Jesus described in the Gospels clearly showed that a relationship with God could only be achieved through saving faith. This involved acknowledgement of sin, repentance, and trusting in Jesus' death and resurrection for forgiveness. But Jesus did not stop at that point. He laid great stress on following God as His disciples. This was going to involve cost, effort and sacrifice. In fact it was to be a complete lifestyle change rather than an 'add on' to what was already experienced. Neither was it an optional extra.

5

The New Testament writers understood this distinctive change, describing it as a 'new' life. The apostle Paul, having himself experienced a revolutionary experience on the Damascus Road, explained it as follows: 'Therefore, if anyone is in Christ, he is a new creation; the old has gone, the new has come!' (2 Corinthians 5:17, NIV1984). This approach was developed in another of his letters:

> You were taught, with regard to your former way of life, to put off your old self, which is being corrupted by its deceitful desires, to be made new in the attitude of your minds; and to put on the new self, created to be like God in true righteousness and holiness.

> (Ephesians 4:22–24)

This teaching in respect of discipleship also impacts us. If we want to walk with God, having an ongoing and deepening relationship with Him, being fruitful and seeing His Kingdom extended, then commitment is vital. We are no longer free to 'do our own thing'. There is no facility regarding taking 'time off' or 'time out'. Self-centred living is not on the agenda. Our focus is to be on Jesus, with our spiritual ears open to what He is saying and our hearts responsive to His prompting. Our minds are to be transformed to know His will.

IN THE BEGINNING

Time is one of the many factors in our new 'job description' as followers of Jesus. God is not ignorant of this dimension. Having first created the celestial bodies by which time could be measured, on the 'fourth day' (Genesis 1:19), He then brought humankind onto the scene. Working in the Garden of Eden in which they were placed, Adam and Eve then chose to disobey God's instructions.

They followed their own preference. But in describing this situation there was one notable feature in respect of time. It was stated: 'Then the man and his wife heard the sound of the LORD God as he was walking in the garden in the cool of the day' (Genesis 3:8). This pointed to God having set a particular time in His overall schedule when He would specifically talk and share with Adam.

This aspect of marking a particular time for focusing on the spiritual aspect of life was subsequently underlined. God's Ten Commandments, given through Moses, gave explicit direction regarding the use of time.

> Remember the Sabbath day by keeping it holy. Six days you shall labour and do all your work, but the seventh day is a sabbath to the LORD your God. On it you shall not do any work, neither you, nor your son or daughter, nor your male or female servant, nor your animals, nor any foreigner residing in your towns. For in six days the LORD made the heavens and the earth, the sea, and all that is in them, but he rested on the seventh day. Therefore the LORD blessed the Sabbath day and made it holy.
>
> (Exodus 20:8–11)

Of all the Commandments this fourth one is the longest in terms of word count (as laid out in our translations such as NIV) and clearly explains the basis on which it was given. A further explanation was given by God to Moses, stating that the Sabbath was a 'sign between me and you for the generations to come' (Exodus 31:12).

A CALL TO PUT GOD FIRST…
Whatever view we may take regarding how that fourth Commandment is now to be applied to ourselves, it underlines the

element of time with regard to our relationship with God. Time was no coincidence or low-profile aspect of God's work. Nor did He intend it to be a peripheral element of His people's relationship with Him. It was, and continues to be, integral to what He does and what He plans for us as His disciples. But the huge problem that we face as twenty-first-century Christians

"..the sheer pace and pressure of life"

that we face as twenty-first-century Christians is the sheer pace and pressure of life. We are bombarded with expectations, schedules, deadlines and 'sell-by' dates. These leave us with little scope and energy for anything except this physical and material dimension in which we operate, dominated by constraints of time.

But God's perspective is very different. It is also not an easy one to grasp in view of those demands that we face. An Old Testament prophet brought a reminder of God's on-going requirement: 'Sow righteousness for yourselves, reap the fruit of unfailing love, and break up your unploughed ground; for it is time to seek the LORD' (Hosea 10:12). The immediate context of that command was God's stipulation that His people (the northern tribes of Israel) stop living self-centred lives. Their focus was entirely upon their own circumstances and pleasures. But it was being stated that the point on the calendar had now been reached when a radical reorientation back to their original relationship with God was required.

...WHICH WAS REPEATED

A similar message was subsequently brought to the Jews who returned from a long period of enforced exile away from their homeland. Haggai's spell as prophet to his people lasted only a few months but it was initiated with a full-on confrontation:

This is what the Lord Almighty says: 'These people say,
"The time has not yet come to rebuild the Lord's house."'
Then the word of the Lord came through the prophet
Haggai: 'Is it a time for you yourselves to be living in
your panelled houses, while this house remains a ruin?'

(Haggai 1:2–4)

This was clearly a rhetorical question. But it was designed to alert
the hearers to a different set of priorities. God needed to be put
first as He had been before.

In this new chapter of the Jews' history, prioritising God was
to be shown by resuming reconstruction of the temple that had
previously been destroyed by invaders. This would, in turn,
facilitate the worship and sacrifice that God had laid down. Up to
this point the people had been totally preoccupied by their own
'home improvements' and lifestyle. Their attitude had been that
God and His work could be slotted into their schedule when and
if it was convenient.

OUR RESPONSE – CONSUMER LIVING?

Fast forward many centuries and we find ourselves in a similar
situation to those Jews. Influenced by the media and the perspective
of those around us, we can be easily sucked back into a self-
absorbed style of living. We can also treat church involvement as
a consumer product – we pick out what we like
and when it's convenient, and in the meantime
get enticed into other things. But those messages
from the Old Testament that it's time to put God
back in first place are also relevant to ourselves.

"..put God back into first place"

Our relationship with God is not a limited,
Sunday-morning-only affair. He wants us to realise that there is

a spiritual dimension to all our activity. This means needing to be wholly committed to Him, learning to have a sensitivity to what He is doing and saying all the time. Meeting with other believers and setting aside specific periods of prayer and Bible reading are means by which this can be enhanced.

The amazing fact is that God's focus and work within our lives is a full-on, 24/7 reality. We may be oblivious to His care and protection but it remains constant even in the hours of sleep. The psalmist points to God's ongoing watch:

> If I rise on the wings of the dawn,
>   if I settle on the far side of the sea,
> even there your hand will guide me,
>   your right hand will hold me fast.
> If I say, 'Surely the darkness will hide me
>   and the light become night around me,'
> even the darkness will not be dark to you;
>   the night will shine like the day,
>   for darkness is as light to you.
>
> (Psalm 139:9–12)

In the light of that statement our only appropriate response is aiming to be God-focused whatever the time on the clock or date on the calendar.

FOR REFLECTION

1. What are the common demands made upon our use of time in the age in which we live? Why is it so difficult to push away such pressures?

2. In what ways could we apply to ourselves, in our present culture, the principle that is behind the fourth Commandment, namely, remembering God?

3. Why, as followers of Jesus, should we be careful about our attitude regarding time?

4. What value may exist in setting aside specific times during each day or week when we try to specifically focus on Jesus by means of talking to Him and reading the Bible?

2

RHYTHM OF LIFE

There is a time for everything, and a season for every activity under heaven.
(Ecclesiastes 3:1, NIV1984)

Some years ago a national newspaper columnist was prompted to write an article about animal behaviour. He described a kingfisher that rendezvoused in the same spot every afternoon at a particular time, a cat that turned up at a bingo hall for human companionship at a set time every evening, and members of other animal species such as badgers, horses and dogs acting in precise ways at exact moments. Further, he described curlews arriving just when the tide turned and how their sought-after mud flats reappeared even though the timing of the tide changed daily. He concluded by asking whether birds and animals have senses which we may have once had but lost long ago.

God pointed out a lack of spiritual sensitivity using a similar comparison. Through the prophet Jeremiah He despaired of His people: 'Even the stork in the sky knows her appointed seasons, and the dove, the swift and the thrush observe the time of their migration. But my people do not know the requirements of the LORD' (Jeremiah 8:7). It is quite clear that, in the area of nature, God put in place a rhythm of time and change. Not only was there evening followed by morning, but other and longer timescale events were instituted: 'As long as the earth endures, seedtime and harvest, cold and heat, summer and winter, day and night will never cease' (Genesis 8:22). These words, initially spoken to Noah after the Flood, remain true today.

But those words describing the rhythm of annual seasons convey an underlying message. The problem is that one of the many consequences of technological change and improved standards of living has been a removal away, by several steps, from the rhythm of nature. As a consequence we are not fully conscious of the shifting seasons that take place.

A PROBLEM

As indicated by that verse from Jeremiah we are not spiritually alert. We fail to embrace the fact that in spiritual growth and activity there is also a timing and rhythm to which we need to be sensitive. Linked to that rhythm there is much 'waiting' time that we need to negotiate. The psalmist drew a parallel between physical and spiritual rhythm in the first psalm: '[The righteous] person is like a tree planted by streams of water, which yields its fruit in season and whose leaf does not wither' (Psalm 1:3). The picture is presented of an ongoing relationship with God, resulting in outward productiveness and involving a period of development.

This maturity is not instantaneous – time is a necessary factor. The book of Proverbs adds:

> Lazy hands make for poverty,
>   but diligent hands bring wealth.
> He who gathers crops in summer is a
>   prudent son,
> but he who sleeps during harvest is a
>   disgraceful son.
>
> (Proverbs 10:4–5)

Paul the apostle continues the theme: 'Let us not become weary in doing good, for at the proper time we will reap a harvest if we do not give up' (Galatians 6:9).

STAGES

Paul also detailed the different spiritual stages that needed to be worked through. He told the Christians in Corinth: 'I planted the seed, Apollos watered it, but God has been making it grow' (1 Corinthians 3:6). These steps are dependent upon each other. They also need to be processed over a period of time. A more sophisticated illustration brings out the same point:

> By the grace God has given me, I laid a foundation as a wise builder, and someone else is building on it. But each one should build with care. For no one can lay any foundation other than the one already laid, which is Jesus Christ. If anyone builds on this foundation using gold, silver, costly stones, wood, hay or straw, their work will be shown for what it is, because the Day will bring it to light.
>
> (1 Corinthians 3:10–13)

This repeated teaching about the processes by which a spiritual impact is made in stages adds an important rider. Going through a process is not sufficient. It needs to be done properly; quality is a vital element.

These 'pictures' that Paul used are still very relevant in our own age. Although inexperienced in the skills of gardening I decided to turn the small patch of green at the back of my house into a vegetable plot. This was a steep learning curve! Seed packets had to be checked for instructions, especially the timing of sowing, planting out and harvesting. The soil needed to be turned over, larger stones removed, and enriching agents added. Finally the seed or seedlings needed to be put in the ground. A long period of dealing with marauding slugs and snails, together with regular watering, then followed. The resultant crop was finally harvested, signalling the end of this rhythm of effort and growth.

A far less physical arduous experience took place at work. Adjacent to the office where I was employed in London was a vacant plot on which a block of flats was being constructed. It was both fascinating and educating to see at close hand the different stages of development that unfolded each day over a period of several months. It was also distracting. Looking at that hive of activity from my desk next to the window was much preferable to looking at work on a computer screen!

DAVID – AN EXAMPLE

Growing and building in our spiritual lives also takes time and effort. When David was being anointed as the next king of Israel by Samuel, he was described as the 'youngest' of Jesse's seven sons. He hadn't even been considered sufficiently mature to receive an invitation to the sacrifice that had been organised as a pretext for the 'selection' process. Instead he had been left out in the fields to tend the sheep. Even though David was subsequently anointed so that 'the Spirit of the LORD came upon [him] in power' (1 Samuel 16:13, NIV1984), he remained in the background. He only came into the limelight when the Israelite army under the reigning monarch, King Saul, was confronted by their Philistine enemies. Goliath, their champion, challenged God's people. But when David, still a 'boy', appeared on the scene, he was the only one who grasped the spiritual dimension of what was taking place. He took up that challenge – but not

" ..grasped the spiritual dimension.."

Saul's armour! Instead he faced the giant on the basis of his trust in God's power. It was this which had previously enabled him to kill any lion or bear that had threatened his flock. Goliath saw that David was only a boy, despised him, and anticipated a resounding conclusion. However, David's training over time in the use of a sling and stone resulted in a totally different outcome. This practised skill and growth of trust in God saw him strike down the giant.

Although David was King Saul's successor, the latter becoming increasingly paranoid and jealous towards him, David refused to 'force the pace' or act prematurely. He was prepared to await God's timing. This showed itself when David, now a fugitive and outlaw on the run from the king, refused on two occasions to take any advantage. One of these was when Saul with his army, hunting for David, was out in the open country. Saul had gone into a cave where, unknown to him, David was hiding with his men. The potential for ending Saul's life was put to David. But he refused to act, and let the king go away unharmed.

Even when King Saul, together with his sons, lost their lives in battle against the Philistines, David refused to take control of the whole kingdom. He only reigned over the tribe of Judah, the other tribes refusing to accept him at that time. Over seven years elapsed before the remainder of Israel called

"..waited on God's timing.." upon David to be their king. He had waited on God's timing and the rhythm that God was working through, before moving into the position for which he had been anointed many years previously. He wrote many of the

psalms, one of which particularly highlights his awareness of time: 'Wait for the LORD and keep his way. He will exalt you to inherit the land' (Psalm 37:34, NIV1984).

CONTEMPORARY SOCIETY

Unfortunately that attitude of waiting and working things through does not sit well in the times in which we live. Contemporary society expects instant results – with minimal input! At the press of a button or keyboard we can access a vast store of information and enact effortless transactions. God's creation and the economy of His Kingdom, where things really matter, present a different set of values. Sowing and reaping, toil and reward, working and waiting are the reality. All involve times and seasons that are overseen and authored by God. All necessitate our awareness and responsiveness.

Modern history also provides examples of leaders emerging after long periods of preparation and waiting. Winston Churchill endured an appalling upbringing in a dysfunctional family. It was the influence of a Godly nanny that initially counteracted the lack of affirmation from his parents. He eventually entered Parliament as an MP in 1900. Eleven years later he was appointed First Lord of the Admiralty, head of the powerful Royal Navy. When this took place it had filled him with excitement and disquiet, leading him to open the Bible by his bed. It opened at random. Churchill read the words:

> Hear, O Israel: Thou art to pass over Jordan this day, to go in to possess nations greater and mightier than thyself, cities great and fenced up to heaven ... Understand therefore this day, that the LORD thy God is he which goeth over before thee ...

> (Deuteronomy 9:1, 3, KJV)

Churchill was said to have drawn great reassurance from this passage. But subsequent military failure in the Dardanelles campaign of World War One led to his resignation. Many years in the political wilderness then followed. Much time was spent by him in studying and researching both past history and the current international scene. But many in the establishment and general public disdained and distrusted him. His advancing years were also against him. Finally those many years of waiting were ended. In May 1940, at a very threatening and dangerous time for the country, he was asked to become Prime Minister. His subsequent galvanising speeches and steadfast spirit were invaluable qualities, developed over years, enabling Great Britain to eventually emerge victorious in World War Two.

GOD'S WORK

A simple parable, recorded only by Mark, further underlines this element of processing as being part of spiritual life:

> He [Jesus] also said, 'This is what the kingdom of God is like. A man scatters seed on the ground. Night and day, whether he sleeps or gets up, the seed sprouts and grows, though he does not know how. All by itself the soil produces

corn – first the stalk, then the ear, then the full gain in the ear. As soon as the grain is ripe, he puts the sickle to it, because the harvest has come.

(Mark 4:26–29)

We have our part to play. This takes our time and effort. However, there is work by which God alone can bring growth, and meanwhile we have to wait for the appropriate seasons to pass. As we do so, we pick up again on the encouragement from Paul that we are not to be 'weary in doing good', or to 'give up' (Galatians 6:9).

FOR REFLECTION

1. In what ways can the world of sport provide a similar picture to that of agriculture and building construction with regard to stages of development needing to be worked through?

2. What encouragement does Psalm 27:13–14 contain in terms of waiting and hoping?

3. What is the value of taking time and effort in preparing for the calling or work which God may want us to undertake?

4. What can be involved in the different seasons through which we have to pass as described in Psalm 1?

3

GOD STEPS INTO TIME

… being made in human likeness. And being found in appearance as
a man, he humbled himself …
(Philippians 2:7–8)

C omputer systems and associated technology are significantly impacting our lives. It is hard to imagine how we would manage without the use of smart phones, iPads, contactless cards and Wi-Fi. These are only a handful of the many vital applications of the silicon chip. How do we react when we find ourselves with a poor signal, the PC goes down, or the battery is low?

Although the above scenario is an inadequate parallel, it helps us to glimpse what it might have been like for the eternal God to step down into time and space. We cannot fully conceive what it meant to Him, just as it is hard for a teenager to imagine life without an iPhone.

But the New Testament describes Jesus, living in eternity, as 'being made in human likeness'. In so doing He lived with a sensitivity to time and as master over it – lessons we need to learn. His coming to earth was not an arbitrary event. The apostle Paul states: 'But when the set time had fully come, God sent his Son, born of a woman, born under the law, to redeem those under the law' (Galatians 4:4–5). His birth was in accordance with the prophecies spoken of Him and timescales that were integral to them.

NOT THE RIGHT TIME

Similarly Jesus' ministry was carried out with an awareness of His Heavenly Father's timing. Attending the wedding at Cana in Galilee, His mother told him of a serious problem: 'They have no more wine.' His response showed perception of the heavenly agenda: 'Dear woman, why do you involve me? ... My time has not yet come' (John 2:4, NIV1984). Although Jesus subsequently worked to turn water into wine, it was performed so that few people were 'in the know'. This, the 'first of his miraculous signs' (v. 11, NIV1984), was not the right time to openly reveal His divinity.

Jesus was alert to the timeframe in which He was to show His Father's love and power. Confronted by His disciples with a man born blind and the question of how this had arisen, His reply revealed a different agenda from that of the questioners... and the timing in which he was operating.

> Neither this man nor his parents sinned ... but this happened so that the work of God might be displayed in his life. As long as it is day, we must do the work of him who sent me. Night is coming, when no-one can work.

> (John 9:3–4, NIV1984)

The crucifixion of Jesus Christ highlighted the element of time. The cry that He uttered, 'It is finished' (John 19:30), signalled not only the completion of God's awesome plan of salvation but that it was being carried out within a set timescale.

IMPLICATIONS

The interaction that Jesus undertook with people in the time-space environment was with an awareness of the restrictions of humanity. His divinity could never be in doubt. On one occasion He replied to a question from Philip, one of His disciples:

> Don't you know me, Philip, even after I have been among you such a long time? Anyone who has seen me has seen the Father. How can you say, 'Show us the Father'? Don't you believe that I am in the Father, and that the Father is in me? The words I say to you are not just my own. Rather, it is the Father, living in me, who is doing his work.

> (John 14:9–10, NIV1984)

Many of those miraculous interventions in which divine power was released involved a time element. This was not only important to those immediately affected by Jesus' touch, but is also relevant to ourselves. Our perspective and understanding of time can be broadened as we not only see what He was doing... but also when! The following sections pick up on some of those occasions which have important implications for us.

DROPPING DOWN...

The first of these miracles involved literal reverberations at the time. This was in the form of the roof falling in! Early in Jesus' ministry He had come home to Capernaum and, faced with a large crowd gathered from far afield, He was preaching to them. Luke adds in his account: 'And the power of the Lord was present for him to heal the sick' (Luke 5:17, NIV1984). Four men decided to bring their paralysed friend on a mat in order to receive healing from Jesus. Such was the size of the crowd that only by opening up the roof and dropping down the mat could this be done. So the roof tiles went! But what also went was Jesus' teaching session. In fact it went immediately. However inconvenient, unscheduled, disruptive and upsetting this dramatic entrance, it did not faze Jesus.

"..it did not faze Jesus"

Whatever may have been on His agenda or in His diary, everything now stopped. It seems that He adjusted to this new scenario without pausing. 'When Jesus saw their faith, he said, "Friend, your sins are forgiven"' (Luke 5:20). The ensuing dialogue between Jesus and the religious leaders who were present soon put the latter in their place. Jesus then demonstrated His power to pronounce forgiveness of sins by telling the paralysed man to get up, pick up his mat and go home... which is exactly what he did.

We need to note that this intervention of Jesus did not necessitate an appointment, coordinated arrangement, or slotting into an itinerary. These four men and their friend simply turned up. The time did not matter to Jesus. In fact their faith in not even waiting until the meeting ended before they approached Jesus was a plus point!

...NO APPOINTMENT NEEDED

Coming and crying out to Jesus in our desperate need is something that can be done at any time, any day. Jesus was operating within the confines of time but He was never mastered or controlled by it. This is still the case. The writer to the Hebrews urged: 'Let us then approach God's throne of grace with confidence, so that we may receive mercy and find grace to help us in our time of need' (Hebrews 4:16). No scheduling is necessary in order to approach Him. Even at the dead of night when the world is asleep we can call to Jesus and experience His intervention.

A prayer was recorded by a royalist commanding officer just before the first major battle of the English Civil War. Sir Jacob Astley in 1642 prayed: 'O Lord, thou knowest how busy I must be this day. If I forget thee, do not thou forget me.' He believed that God would not forget him whatever the time of day – relationship with Him was a not on an appointment-only basis.

DROPPING OFF...

That first aspect of time in respect of Christ's ministry showed that He was not tied down by it. The second aspect builds on that perspective: He was not put off by it. 'Some time later' we read that Jesus went up to Jerusalem and to a pool named Bethesda. This was a place where a 'great number of disabled people used to lie – the blind, the lame, the paralysed' (John 5:3). In particular there was a man lying there who had been an invalid for 38 years. The narrative specifically states that Jesus 'learned that he had been in this condition for a long time' (John 5:6). It suggests that Jesus checked to find out who had been ill the longest... and then showed His compassion and power to the most chronic case.

That long-term invalid had evidently 'dropped off' everyone else's 'radar'. No one was now willing to help him into the pool when the water had from time to time, it seems, been supernaturally stirred. Some manuscripts of Scripture explain that an angelic presence disturbed the waters so that whoever then got into the pool first was cured. But this man had not dropped off Jesus' horizon. Nor was Christ put off by the long timespan of what must have been 38 miserable and hopeless years. At Jesus' command the man was healed, 'picked up his mat and walked' (John 5:8–9).

This was not an isolated example of time not proving an obstacle in Jesus bringing wholeness into people's lives and bodies. A woman who had been suffering from bleeding for 12 years came and touched Jesus' cloak. It was stated that she had 'suffered a great deal under the care of many doctors and had spent all she had, yet instead of getting better she grew worse' (Mark 5:26). Her action resulted in the release of Christ's healing power. An even longer period of suffering, 18 years, had been experienced by a crippled woman. She was bent over and could not straighten up at all. But Jesus saw her in the synagogue where He was teaching, called her forward and spoke healing into her body. 'Then he put his hands on her, and immediately she straightened up and praised God' (Luke 13:13).

...BUT NO SELL-BY DATE

The Gospel writers included in their accounts the healing of many people, most of whom, it is likely, had illnesses or disability that had existed for some time. The three examples above (and that of the blind man) showed that the length of time over which a condition existed did not prevent Jesus bringing healing. The advanced ages of Zechariah and Elizabeth (Luke 1) and, many centuries previously, Abraham and Sarah (Genesis 22) were not a barrier to God's power enabling them to have children. That is one reason why Jesus taught us that we 'ought always to pray, and not to faint' (Luke 18:1, KJV), 'should always pray and not give up' (NIV). Perhaps we are too easily deterred by the passing of time when prayer seems unanswered and situations remain unchanged. God wants us to trust Him to intervene even though a long period of time might have passed. We should not think of our situations being like tins of baked beans with a 'sell-by' date!

For centuries the Bible had been a hidden and unread book, written in Latin and only open to a small well-educated elite. But those many years of obscurity were not an insurmountable obstacle to God's Word eventually being made available to anyone who could read. Within a relatively short period of time a number of key factors contributed to this change. These included the introduction of the printing press, the emergence of English as a respected language, the Reformation, and the separation of England from the Roman Church. It was also the bravery of men like John Wycliffe and then William Tyndall that eventually led to King James I formally authorising publication of the Bible in English.

DROPPING IN...

The above snapshots of Jesus' ministry show Him responding in power to situations where time was a major factor. But there were also specific occasions when He clearly took the initiative. Jesus was 'dropping in' on people at a time that they did not expect but which was important in terms of their spiritual life. This was certainly the case with the Samaritan woman whom He met at a well where she had come to draw water. The Gospel writer specified the time: 'It was about the sixth

"..a time they did not expect.."

hour' (John 4:6, NIV1984). This meant that it was about 12 noon. Being the hottest part of day, and drawing water (and carrying it home) being an arduous task, this was not the normal time for this activity.

As subsequently revealed, this woman's domestic affairs probably explained her wanting to avoid contact with neighbours by drawing water when no one else was likely to be around. Except that Jesus wanted to meet her. With no one else present He shared with her the truth about real worship and relationship with God. This encounter, at this unusual time, changed this woman's life.

...AT AN UNUSUAL HOUR

The disciples of Jesus, who eventually turned up to find Him alone with the Samaritan woman, themselves had a spiritual encounter at an unusual time. Only theirs was not in the blazing sunshine but in the dead of night, in a boat battling against a wild storm. Jesus had instructed them to go ahead of Him to the other side of the Lake of Galilee. Meanwhile He had dismissed the crowd who had previously been miraculously fed with a few loaves and fishes. He then went up a mountainside to pray alone. It was when the disciples' boat was engulfed by the waves that He went out to them, walking on water. This was 'during the fourth watch of the night' (Matthew 14:25, NIV1984). That would equate to a time between three and six o'clock in the morning. The reaction to seeing Jesus on the water was one of fear... and, for Peter, of audacious faith. The latter asked Jesus to confirm His identity by telling him to come to Him on the water. Jesus did so, but when Peter took his eyes off Him and saw the wind, he began to sink. Jesus' comment as

He reached out to rescue him was of pointing out his 'little faith' (v. 31). As was the case with the other disciples whom He had directed to 'take courage' (v. 27), He wanted trust to be exercised.

'Dropping in' at the time that Jesus did was part of that important lesson for those disciples in the boat. It was also a factor when Jesus met Zacchaeus. Although the actual time of day was not recorded, it was a situation that this tax collector had not anticipated. But it allowed sufficient time for Jesus to visit him: 'I must stay at your house today' (Luke 19:5). As with all these other examples, the result was spiritual change being experienced.

Whatever the page in the diary, Jesus still wants to intervene in our lives. He stepped into our world over 2,000 years ago and continues to work in our situations, although confined by time, to show His love and power.

FOR REFLECTION

1. How does our awareness of God working within the confines of our time-space dimension help us sense a closer relationship with Him?

2. Why, subconsciously or otherwise, might we feel that we can only experience the closeness of Jesus at certain times and in certain places?

3. What steps could we take to realise that we can know Jesus with us at any time or place?

4. What might contribute to us feeling that too much time has passed regarding particular situations and that therefore God cannot now act?

5. What steps could we take to understand that God may have a different perspective on situations which we feel have passed their 'sell-by' date?

4

THE RIGHT PLACE AND TIME

Just as Gehazi was telling the king how Elisha had restored the dead to life, the woman whose son Elisha had brought back to life came to appeal to the king for her house and land.

(2 Kings 8:5)

'Would you like some free tickets?' I was busily working at my desk when a colleague in the office approached me with this question. He had been looking for people who might be interested in this offer of tickets to watch a football match the next day. Since the team in question was Leyton Orient (a struggling team in the lower levels of the English Football League) there were no takers! Then he saw me, a backslidden O's supporter! So, being in the right place at the right time, I took up the offer. As a consequence I witnessed a creditable 0–0 result against strong opposition.

APPEARING ON THE SCENE

Many of the ways in which God works in our lives can arise from us 'being in the right place at the right time'. Such was the experience of the 'Shunammite woman'. She had been blessed by God in having her dead son restored back to life through

Elisha (see 2 Kings 4:8–36). But she had then been instructed by the prophet to leave the country on account of a pending famine. This had lasted seven years. Upon return she needed to approach the king in order to beg for the return of her house and land. Unbeknown to her, the servant of Elisha had been recounting to the king, at the latter's request, the great things that the man of God had done. Just as he was describing how Elisha had restored the dead to life, this woman appeared on the scene! The servant immediately identified her and her son as being the central characters in that miracle. The woman confirmed the details and then the king assigned an official to her case. Everything was to be restored to her, including the 'back' money that was due since she had left the country (see 2 Kings 8:1–6). God worked in this amazing 'coincidence' to enable her to receive everything back.

This is not an isolated biblical example. Gideon and his companion arrived on the edge of the enemy camp as directed by God. This was just as two soldiers were in discussion about a dream. One of them had dreamt of a round loaf of barley bread coming tumbling into their camp, striking and overturning a tent. Their interpretation, overhead by Gideon, was that the dream foretold victory for God's people (Judges 7:9–14). This galvanised Gideon into action, having faith to mobilise the little group of 300 men whom God had organised around him. They were used by God to overcome this invading enemy horde.

UNEXPECTED ARRIVAL

Preceding these accounts, the well-known record of Joseph featured the element of time in the narrative of his troubles. It can be easily missed. In the opening scenes Joseph's jealous brothers grabbed hold of him out in the wild countryside and threw him into an empty water cistern. The indications are that their intention was to get him 'off their backs'... permanently. Many years later they referred back to this event when talking among themselves while in the courts of Egypt. They remembered Joseph's response to their action: 'We saw how distressed he was when he pleaded with us for his life' (Genesis 42:21). What saved Joseph from this premature end was the unexpected arrival over the horizon of a caravan of Ishmaelites coming from Gilead, bound for Egypt. One of the brothers saw an alternative solution to their 'problem'. The others agreed, and so Joseph was sold as a slave and ended up in Egypt.

This would not have taken place had not this caravan appeared just as the brothers sat down to eat before making an end to Joseph. The latter might not have understood what was going on or been happy with this turn of events, orchestrated by God though unseen. But it was a major factor in what was to follow (see Genesis 37:23–28).

RUNNING AND TRAVELLING

In the New Testament the evangelist Philip was instructed by God to leave an area where many miracles were being experienced. He was to go south on the road leading into the desert. Seeing a chariot in that desolate spot, he was then told by God's Spirit to approach it. So he ran to the Ethiopian official's chariot just at the point when this traveller was reading from the Old Testament prophecy of Isaiah. In particular he had come to the verses describing the 'suffering Servant' (Acts 8:30–33; Isaiah 53). It was this

"So he ran...just at the point.."

passage that Philip was able to use to tell him 'the good news about Jesus'. As a consequence the official became a Believer, being baptised in some water when they came across it by the desert road.

Later in the Acts of the Apostles there is an account of a God-fearing Gentile, Cornelius, sending a deputation to Peter. This was just when the apostle had come to realise, through a dramatic daytime vision, that God's salvation extended beyond the boundaries of Israel. Peter was 'wondering about the meaning' of this vision (Acts 10:17) when those visitors arrived at his front door. As Peter subsequently explained, it was against the religious law for a Jew to associate with a Gentile or visit him. But God's revelation just at that time had prompted Peter to accept the invitation to travel to Caesarea. He subsequently spoke to everyone whom Cornelius had gathered together at his house, a large gathering of relatives and close friends. Peter's message was about Jesus, His death and resurrection. But it seems that God wasn't waiting for the 'punchline' or any 'altar call'! It is recorded that while Peter was still speaking, the Holy Spirit came down on his listeners. They all spoke in tongues and praised God in such a way that Peter then directed them to be baptised as true Believers.

AMY JOHNSON...

Even secular history records the intervention of God at key moments in people's lives. Although aviation is now a commonplace mode of travel in comfortable and safe airliners, that is only a relatively recent achievement. The pioneers of the first part of the last century blazed trails which are now generally forgotten. One of these was a woman named Amy Johnson. Her plan was to fly from England to Australia – in a small and fragile aeroplane with no radio, radar or ground control facilities to oversee her flight. Even for contemporary travellers this is quite a long and demanding flight. Back in 1930 it was the equivalent to spaceflight today. This was especially the case as Amy was flying alone in a single-engine biplane with limited fuel capacity. So her aim was to make the journey – in her De Havilland 'Gipsy Moth' which she named Jason – by means of short 'hops'. She would land to refuel at predesignated aerodromes. This was fine while flying over the landmasses of Europe and the Middle East, but beyond that area were stretches of ocean.

At one point Amy decided to risk a shortcut over the Java Sea. But when out of sight of land, she was confronted with unexpected heavy rain and thick clouds. She described being unable to go on or turn back. All she could do was circle round and round. But she also prayed, something she stated that she did at the start of every morning's flight even though not classing herself as religious. Then, just as she was about to give up, the sun burst through the cloud. Immediately she saw the opportunity to dart into the sudden gap that now appeared in the haze. She headed for the coast that she then saw ahead of her. The timing of the change in conditions enabled her to complete that leg of the journey to Java, before eventually flying to Port Darwin, Australia, after 20 eventful days.

Apparently Amy Johnson had often spoken of guardian angels watching over her throughout her journey. The undoubted intervention of God at that time over the sea was a dramatic experience of Him at work in the right place at the right time.

...AND OTHER MECHANICAL ISSUES

Fast forward another generation from Amy Johnson and car travel was then the norm for many people in Britain. The year 1948 saw the first production of over one million Morris Minors (or '1000s'), often viewed as a quintessential British vehicle. Most have now rusted away, although a significant number are still seen motoring along quieter (and slower) stretches of road. Mine has been one of them! I bought a 'used' Minor on account of its economy, ease of maintenance and reliability. These qualities have proved very useful. However, on one occasion a particular problem arose. Having driven up to Suffolk from London, I noticed that the ignition light on the control panel remained glowing. This was not good news. Essentially it meant that the battery, normally charged up by the dynamo as the car raced along (!), was not actually being powered up. I was therefore faced with a choice. Either I risk driving down to the south coast as I had planned within that next week, or try and get the fault diagnosed and rectified. Having no time for the latter, I decided to undertake that further journey – the car seemed to be quite 'happy' otherwise.

The subsequent drive was well over 100 miles. Being in 'prayer mode' while driving, I tried not to look in the direction of the dashboard ignition light. I arrived safely and without any problem, enjoying a few days' camping in the New Forest. The return journey took a slightly different route in order to avoid both central London and the motorway. As I was driving along a road which skirted the latter, I felt 'prompted' to stop for some petrol. When I got back into the car the engine refused to start – the battery was finally flat after over 300 miles of non-charging. But I was delighted! God had kept the car going until I was returning home, stopped off-road in a service station with full facilities. I was also within distance of the specialist garage that would be able to provide the necessary 'TLC' (tender loving care). A phone call to the vehicle rescue organisation... and, apart from the ignominious necessity of having the car hauled onto a low-loader, everything had worked out well. The problem may have been self-inflicted, but God had intervened at just the right time and place so that the car eventually stopped when causing the least hassle.

OUR RESPONSIBILITY

We can be encouraged that God is working in all our circumstances. This means that, whether we know what's happening or are completely oblivious to events, He can ensure that we are in the right place at the right time. This is so that His purposes are carried out for our own lives and for others. But we still have a responsibility. Our part is to be sensitive to His 'nudges' and 'promptings'. This is a factor that is particularly evident in biblical accounts. Like many Godly people in the Scriptures, we need to be open to His Spirit, and to respond so that we are where we need to be, at the appropriate time... even in the 'ordinary' routine of our daily chores and responsibilities.

FOR REFLECTION

1. What's the value in reflecting on the past in order to pick out timely (and unforeseen) interventions by God such as Joseph experienced?

2. Why should we be sensitive to God's 'promptings' and 'nudges' (as with Peter and Philip) even though they may not make sense?

3. In being responsive to God's 'nudges', what is the value in not prevaricating – either in terms of not acting straight away or not being diligent in asking God for clarification or confirmation?

4. What encouragement can we derive from knowing that God is able to intervene in a timely way in the events of our lives even though we may not be aware of the 'big picture' or the implications of what's going on?

5

SEIZING OPPORTUNITIES

And who knows but that you have come to your royal position for such a time as this?
(Esther 4:14)

Malta is a popular holiday destination in the Mediterranean. It's a small island, 17 miles long and 9 miles at its widest point. But it enjoys a climate and culture, together with scenery, that appeals to tourists. However, back in 1940 there were visitors of a distinctly unwanted category. Warplanes from the German and Italian air forces flew overhead to unleash waves of bombs in an effort to subdue the allies desperately clinging to this vital isolated outpost. In military terms the island was like an unsinkable aircraft carrier anchored 60 miles from Italian territory. In the other direction lay North Africa where the German Afrika Corps was building up its forces, intent on attacking and overrunning Egypt. Malta was positioned to provide a base for ships, submarines and aircraft to disrupt the supply of military materials to that Corps.

The commander in charge of Malta at this time was Lieutenant General Sir William Dobbie. He had actually retired from military service after a long and distinguished career. Not only had he fought on the Western Front in World War One but he had subsequently been given charge of operations during the 1929 Palestine Emergency. He then took responsibility for planning the fortifications of Singapore, though a lack of funds prevented implementation – with tragic results.

Following his retirement, and with the outbreak of World War Two, Dobbie offered his services to the military. In April 1940 he was consequently given the opportunity to be appointed as Governor of Malta. Two months later Italy declared war on Great Britain, and Malta suffered the first of many air raids. The island was ill-prepared to withstand any attack. But Dobbie's indomitable Christian faith galvanised both armed and civilian personnel in Malta when under this intense and prolonged bombardment. He never failed to take opportunities to share and proclaim his vibrant commitment to God and belief in the Bible. This was something that he had previously done when in Palestine, sending a message to his servicemen reminding them of the spiritual significance of the place where they had been posted. After two years in Malta he was invalided back to Britain, having laid the foundations for the eventual lifting of the siege of the island.

CONFRONTATION

The Bible describes many characters who had an impact arising from opportunities being seized. The book of Esther is an account of a Jewish girl who was amazingly installed as queen in a heathen court. Her ethnic background remained undisclosed. But when her exiled people were threatened with annihilation through a royal edict, her uncle confronted her with the fact that her status would not exempt her from the same fate. He followed this with a challenge: 'And who knows but that you have come to your royal position for such a time as this?' (Esther 4:14). All that had previously taken place in her life had prepared her for this particular time and opportunity. She therefore took the step, literally, of going into the presence of the king-emperor, although not officially summoned. This risked his displeasure and her execution. But the king received her and she was able to initiate action which ultimately saved the Jewish people at that time.

OUT OF THE BLUE

Nehemiah was another character in the Old Testament who seized an opportunity to impact events. Like Esther he was working in an environment where power was being exercised. But unlike her, he was simply facilitating rather than influencing it… until one day something changed. Nehemiah had previously received dreadful news of the plight of his fellow Jews back in Jerusalem and the ruined state of the city walls. Although he was many miles away in exile, he was devastated.

Nehemiah was unable to disguise these emotions, and the king-emperor noticed his expression. Fearful in case the king took exception to his sadness, he explained what had caused it. Out of the blue the king asked the question: 'What is it you want?' Nehemiah seized this amazing, God-given, opportunity. He requested leave of absence to go to Jerusalem. He also asked for letters of safe conduct and authorisation for building material to be supplied. This was the starting point for God's restoration of His people back to a rebuilt capital city and temple of worship.

LOW PROFILE

The New Testament account of the birth of Jesus includes events arising from similar, unforeseen, circumstances. However, the people who seized them had a much lower profile than either Esther or Nehemiah. But that didn't stop such opportunities

41

arising... or being taken. The same is true for ourselves – openings do not arise because of status or being a celebrity. The shepherds watching over their flocks were certainly not everyone's Facebook 'Friend'. Yet they were suddenly confronted in the dead of night by a host of angelic beings who were praising God for His intervention in sending Jesus Christ as a baby in Bethlehem. When the angels left them, the shepherds responded to this

"..suddenly confronted.." news by seeing – and seizing – an opportunity: 'Let's go to Bethlehem and see this thing that has happened, which the Lord has told us about' (Luke 2:15).

The baby Jesus was subsequently brought to the temple to be presented to the Lord as prescribed by the Law of Moses. While there, a priest named Simeon was prompted by the Holy Spirit to go into the temple courts and took the opportunity to speak prophetically over Jesus. Similarly an aged prophetess named Anna, 'coming up to them at that very moment' (Luke 2:38), recognised the significance of what was happening. She consequently saw the opening to share the good news of the Messiah 'to all who were looking forward to the redemption of Jerusalem'.

PERSECUTION – AN OPPORTUNITY

Many of the accounts recorded in the subsequent Acts of the Apostles include this element of 'seizing' opportunities. The apostle Peter took the opportunity to preach to thousands of listeners on the Day of Pentecost on the back of an accusation that the disciples were drunk (Acts 2:14). Peter and John were used by God to bring healing to a lame man at the temple gate when going up to pray at a particular time (Acts 3:1–6). Followers of Jesus, scattered to places well outside of Jerusalem on account of persecution, saw openings to preach about Jesus in their new locations. Philip was one of these followers, preaching and performing miraculous signs in Samaria, with the result that this seized opportunity caused 'great joy in that city' (Acts 8:4–8).

SURPRISE

Opportunities form part of the fabric of life whatever our circumstances, with time being integral to them. There are a number of aspects which can be drawn from the above biblical examples and which are relevant to ourselves. The first of these is that opportunities often arise unexpectedly and surprisingly. While there might be an inkling or suspicion of something happening, the general effect is that we can't plan or engineer such an opening. They arise outside of our control… we can't put a note in our diary (or electronic equivalent) to prepare us for their occurrence.

This element of being out of our control is actually true of life itself. While we can plan to a certain extent, the exact future is unknown. That's why the book of Proverbs advises: 'Do not boast about tomorrow, for you do not know what a day may bring forth' (Proverbs 27:1, NIV1984). In the New Testament we read: 'Now listen, you who say, "Today or tomorrow we will go to this or that city, spend a year there, carry on business and make money." Why, you do not even know what will happen tomorrow' (James 4:13–14). While the writer of Proverbs also has advice about planning being a wise action to take, such plans are to be committed to the Lord (16:3). It's further pointed out that the end result is in God's hands: 'Many are the plans in a person's heart, but it is the LORD's purpose that prevails' (Proverbs 19:21).

All of this underlines the fact that although opportunities are possibly a complete surprise to us, they are not a surprise to God! Indeed He is the one that is not only aware of them but in some way controls them. My own work in preparing spiritual growth and Bible study material for a wider audience has been a learning curve in that respect. Situations have unexpectedly arisen on the back of these efforts. On one particular Saturday I was trying to summon up some inspiration when the phone interrupted my thoughts. It was an unexpected invitation to facilitate a day retreat at a Christian centre that I had previously visited. I had left the managers a couple of books as a resource, and when a scheduled speaker pulled out they were prompted to contact me.

SPOTTED

But opportunities sometimes also need to be spotted. They may not be obvious or clear-cut. So this requires being alert to what's happening and recognising possibilities that may exist, however slight. The problem that most of us have, much of the time, is that we are so engaged or preoccupied that opportunities pass by unnoticed. As we shall also see, they might also have a short 'shelf-life'. This means that if not identified and acted upon within a period of time, they may be gone, never to re-emerge. The apostle Paul admonished the Christians at Ephesus to be alert in this respect on account of the times in which they were living: 'Be very careful, then, how you live – not as unwise but as wise, making the most of every opportunity, because the days are evil' (Ephesians 5:15–16).

In the context of being alert the Old Testament records a period in the history of Israel when David was king – but only over Judah. He had been in that position for a period as the remaining tribes had not considered it appropriate for him to reign over the rest of the nation. It was a season of considerable uncertainty and instability. But among those who sided with David with a view to installing him as overall king was a particular group who discerned what was going on: 'men of Issachar, who understood the times and knew what Israel should do' (1

44

Chronicles 12:32, NIV1984). It's not only a mass of confusing circumstances that can prevent us from spotting openings. Thomas Edison once observed: 'Opportunity is missed by most people because it is dressed in overalls and looks like work.'

This aspect of spotting opportunities can arise in a particularly important area of concern to many Christians. It is with respect to hearing God speak to us individually. Doubts may surface as to whether we have missed opportunities to hear God's voice and whether these are limited in some way. However, we are assured that God takes account of our frailty and shortcomings – He actually speaks to us more than we are ready to listen. But practical action on our part can help! This can entail keeping a Bible, pen and paper to hand at all times if possible... or the technological equivalent. This means that we can be ready to note down anything that God might be bringing to our attention, wherever we may be. Certainly when at church services, meetings or small groups it is a good idea to come prepared to record what we sense God is saying. It's a way of indicating to Him that we are open to opportunities to hear Him speak. On one occasion, during a long train journey and suitably armed with Bible, pen and paper, I arrived at my destination with a list of things that I'd sensed God was bringing to my attention that I'd not previously picked up. Being proactive is something that Paul underlined on one occasion: 'Be on your guard; stand firm in the faith; be courageous; be strong. Do everything in love' (1 Corinthians 16:13–14).

"..opportunities to hear Him.."

STEPPING OUT

Thirdly, opportunities not only need to be recognised but also need a positive response. This is likely to mean stepping out in faith. Because such openings can be unexpected, a degree of unpreparedness is probably going to exist. So trusting in God for what lies ahead is going to be important. Hanging around and wanting more time to weigh things up may not be an option.

On one occasion, while I was still working as a junior manager in a high-profile government department, I was summoned to a meeting. My boss had gathered our team together to unexpectedly announce that volunteers were needed for a spell of detached duty at another office. Because of the considerably increased commuting time that this would involve, and the anticipated low level of support for the work itself, I was not willing to pursue this opening. But God had other ideas! Feeling a distinct unease about not taking this up, I sensed that this was God's means of 'nudging' me to volunteer. This needed to be done quickly as there was a deadline to be met. So, despite reservations, I stepped out and took the opportunity. Although the required work was not easy and very 'hands on', it ended up as one of the most rewarding and satisfying projects in which I was involved. I really sensed God's help, presence and blessing during that time.

SEASON

The final aspect to be noted in respect of opportunities and the time element is that the latter may consist of a limited period. The expression 'window of opportunity' is sometimes used in that context. It underlines the fact that an opening may not be around for any length of time and therefore needs to be spotted and acted upon. A sombre account is recorded in the Acts of the Apostles regarding Felix, a Roman governor, who failed to realise the eternal significance of this limitation. Having previously heard Paul's defence against accusations from the Jewish religious leaders, he summoned Paul again:

He sent for Paul and listened to him as he spoke about faith in Christ Jesus. As Paul discoursed on righteousness, self-control and the judgment to come, Felix was afraid and said, 'That's enough for now! You may leave. When I find it convenient, I will send for you ['... when I have a convenient season, I will send for thee', KJV].

(Acts 24:24–25)

There is no record of such a 'convenient season' arising for Felix again. The opportunity to respond to God through Paul's preaching never apparently arose again in the same way. Although Felix 'sent for him frequently and talked with him' (v. 26), it is simply recorded that when two years had passed he was succeeded by Porcius Festus. We hear of no positive response to the gospel message.

Paul himself highlighted the link between 'opportunity' and 'time'. When writing to the Colossian Christians he instructed them: 'Be wise in the way you act towards outsiders; make the most of every opportunity ['... redeeming the time', KJV]' (Colossians 4:5). The Greek word for 'time' in this context is *kairos* and means 'opportune, set, or appointed time'. It is the definitive time, the proper time for action; it is not open-ended.

The sense of having limited openings for action has had many practical implications in the area of Christian work. When the USSR disintegrated in the 1990s there were new opportunities to share the gospel with Russians and other nationalities in the former Soviet bloc. But it was sensed that this 'open door' might not exist for long. The Gospel Printing Mission based in east London was one group who recognised this possibility. Action was therefore quickly taken to prepare and print as many gospel tracts and teaching booklets as possible for Christians and churches in that part of Europe and Asia. These were sent out following many requests that were received. Sadly the number of contacts that were made as a result of posting out material declined as time progressed. This was the result of a gradual clampdown by the authorities, action which showed the necessity of prompt response when God provides opportunities.

The phrase 'Carpe diem' encapsulates this connection between opportunity and time: 'Seize the day.' Paul, again, recognised the way in which God worked within these parameters. He wrote on one occasion: 'But I will stay on at Ephesus until Pentecost, because a great door for effective work has opened to me' (1 Corinthians 16:9). As a preacher from the USA once said: 'Opportunities are the most that you get.' So let's keep looking out for them, and taking them up when the time is right, with God's help!

FOR REFLECTION

1. How can we adopt a more open attitude in our routines and responsibilities to the unexpected opportunities that God may bring to us?

2. What practical steps can we take to spot God-given opportunities which we might otherwise miss? What do you think Thomas Edison was trying to underline in the quotation in this chapter?

3. What factors can make 'stepping out' an obstacle, and what provisions has God made so that we can overcome them?

4. How can we be sensitive to the 'seasons' in which God is particularly working and our involvement in them?

6

LESSONS FOR LIFE

Teach us to number our days, that we may gain a heart of wisdom.
(Psalm 90:12)

The British Prime Minister, Herbert Asquith, once pondered that youth would be an ideal state if it came a bit later in life! This underlined the need for vitality and an outside-the-box approach to be put alongside maturity gained from experience. In the supercharged pace of life that most people – Christians included – seem to pursue, there seems little time to pause for mature reflection. Even needing time to plan and make sound choices seems rarely acknowledged as important.

OUTSIDE OF TIME

Psalm 90, noted as 'A prayer of Moses the man of God', was written in a pre-technological age. However, it highlights several factors relating to time that are relevant to us all, whether or not we know how to work an iPhone or Kindle! They are also words born out of hard-won experience. Moses' starting point is to remind us that God is outside of time: 'from everlasting to everlasting you are God' (v. 2). God, however, is also our 'dwelling-place [or refuge] throughout all generations' (v. 1). Our minds cannot grasp the meaning of eternity. But it is reassuring to know that through whatever times we may pass, God is ever-present and close to us. This introduction points to a fixed feature of life. God has seen the wheel 'reinvented' over many centuries – but He Himself doesn't change!

The second underlining factor brought out in this psalm regarding time is that our days on this earth are both fragile and fleeting. This is in marked contrast to God for whom 'a thousand years ... are like a day that has just gone by, or like a watch in the night' (v. 4). We are described as 'dust' (v. 3) and likened to the new grass of the morning which is dry and withered by evening (vv. 5–6), a repeated theme of the Bible. One of the big problems that we face in this generation is concentrating on the 'now'. There is much focus on finding immediate answers, fulfilment and enjoyment. Living for the moment leaves little space to take 'tomorrow' into account or the fact that some day will be our last on this earth. People only seem concerned with Facebook postings, celebrity status and constant texting interaction. This doesn't leave much time or energy for more important matters... which caused Moses to move into top gear!

SIN – A HUGE FACTOR

The fact of sin may not seem relevant to time. But Moses, thirdly, underlined the sin in this world and in ourselves as being a huge factor. It has a strong bearing on our limited lifespan – 80 years, 'if we have the strength' (v. 10, NIV1984) – and the quality of those years. The latter are described as consisting of 'trouble and sorrow' (v. 10). The Genesis account of creation highlighted the presence of sin as actually being the cause of toil and physical death.

Other incidents in the Bible suggest that premature death can arise because of particular spiritual failure. Both Ananias and his wife Sapphira lied to church leaders regarding the amount they had received from sold property subsequently presented as a gift to the church. When separately confronted by this deceit, they each fell dead. Not surprisingly, 'Great fear seized the whole church and all who heard about these events' (Acts 5:11)! Paul wrote to the Christians at Corinth to rebuke them for their behaviour and attitude, especially when meeting for the Lord's Supper. This, he stated, was an issue which had meant that some of their number were weak, sick and had 'fallen asleep' (meaning that they had died; 1 Corinthians 11:27–30). So even if we do not take a long lifespan for granted, we may wrongly assume that good health and resources will be retained. The spiritual quality of our lives – our close walk with God – might, in some way, affect how many days we spend on this earth and the limitations in which they are lived.

A PIVOTAL POINT – TIME MANAGEMENT

The request that Moses then puts to God as recorded in this psalm is a pivotal point: 'Teach us to number our days, that we may gain a heart of wisdom' (v. 12). This is regarded as an appeal for help in using time wisely. It's raised in the light of what has previously been stated about God and our sin. We might think that 'Time Management' courses, so often featured in contemporary corporate and organisational training schemes, are a new innovation. But here it's being raised by Moses a very long time ago! Importantly it's in the context of our spiritual well-being.

Moses knew that he needed help with time management... and that God was the best Person to teach it! His request comes immediately on the back of the statement that 'anger' was the divine response to the thoughtless attitude of people towards time (v. 11).

ACKNOWLEDGEMENT – FINITE TIME

So what are the lessons for life that have a spiritual impact and which we need to be taught with regard to time? What's on God's 'Time Management' syllabus? What is the practical application that affects us in the twenty-first century? Top of the list would simply be the need to 'number our days'. We have to acknowledge that our time on earth is finite... as well as fleeting and fragile. This means that we will not have the time, energy or resources to do all the things that we want to do or that others might expect of us. Such a realisation might be hard to accept. But it should focus our attention on what we are doing and the respective value of those activities.

ASSESSMENT – STEPPING BACK

Implicit in this 'numbering' is the need to assess. This second item on the syllabus means weighing up what tasks and responsibilities we aim to pursue. We then have to decide what is essential as distinct from being a nice idea. Taking a step back and viewing the 'big picture' (with God's help) forms part of this assessment. We might want other people to share this review with us. Over a period of time, I've had suggestions thrown in my direction about undertaking more formal theological training. Clearly this is a positive step to consider. I've consequently mulled over the various repercussions such as the energy needed for such sustained studying, the financial outlay and intellectual ability. In the light of these and other criteria I've decided not to go ahead. Perhaps my view might change in the future. But I'm satisfied that my current level of commitment in other areas simply has a higher priority.

Sometimes, of course, God specifically intervenes in this assessment process! When working in the civil service I was put forward for promotion. My bosses felt that I had the necessary qualities for this higher grade. However, the interviewing board was of a different opinion. I failed the selection process and at the time I found this hard to accept. But as I observed the increased demands on those with that greater responsibility as time progressed, I recognised God's overruling in that outcome. It meant that existing commitments, particularly church involvement, could be properly maintained and enhanced.

Clearly, establishing what God wants us to do with our time and energy in the particular season through which we are passing is an important action. The request at the end of Psalm 90, 'establish the work of our hands for us' (v. 17), underlines that time needs to be given to what God has specifically called us to undertake. In the New Testament the apostle Paul indicated this need to identify and focus on specific tasks: 'With this in mind, we constantly pray for you, that our God may count you worthy of his calling, and that by his power he may bring to fruition your every desire for goodness and your every deed prompted by faith' (2 Thessalonians 1:11).

ACCOUNTABILITY – OUR RESPONSIBILITY

There are clearly certain 'givens' that are likely to arise in assessing how our time is used. These might include responsibilities such as family support, personal health, facilitating an income, and spiritual devotions. But ascertaining these, having taken a step back to see the big picture, leads to a third item on God's syllabus which is accountability. In one sense the psalmist, in writing about asking for God's help, was implying that he wanted to be accountable before God. But as in the case of our general conduct, self-control and self-accountability need to be part of this overall package. We cannot 'offload' all our responsibility. It's certainly good and wise to have others with whom we can discuss and share these important issues. But when the 'rubber hits the road' we have to shoulder the final decisions that have to be made in managing time.

"Technology
.. leaves us ..
little excuse"

So in the context of accountability there is the need for some very practical action – to record and review. 'Record' refers to keeping a diary of planned meetings, events, things 'to do' and dates by which completion is required. This will probably mean a greater degree of sophistication than scribbled notes on a kitchen calendar! It will also entail discipline in noting details when they first come to light. But then that record needs to be systematically and regularly reviewed. This is to ensure that appropriate action is taken and preparation takes place. Technology now leaves us with little excuse for not being able to access pocket-sized gadgets to manage all of this… unless there are problems with technophobia!

When I moved on from working in the civil service this form of accountability, I soon found, was crucial in keeping organised. I had previously kept a separate diary at work, backed up by colleagues reminding me of meetings and courses. This was clearly limited to my office regime. But on account of various

God-orchestrated circumstances, I was now, in essence, working in a freelance capacity. This was a whole new world! It was also very fluid and unstructured. I realised that self-discipline at this basic level of recording and reviewing was essential to keep me focused on various and diverse activities.

ASKING – WHAT WE NEED FROM GOD

In view of these different pressures regarding time and needing to manage it wisely, it's not surprising how the psalm ends. Moses asks for God's compassion and mercy in all that's going on. He reminds God of the days in which affliction has come and the years of trouble that have been seen. In the context of such negative experiences, whatever the particular details, he specifically pleads for change. He wants to know God's 'unfailing love', and that this is an ongoing experience ('Satisfy us in the morning', v. 14). This links up with the declaration recorded in Lamentations that God's compassions never fail: 'They are new every morning; great is your faithfulness' (Lamentations 3:23).

This final lesson relates to essentially asking for God's intervention. Like the others it needs to be fleshed out in the light of our individual responsibilities. We are living in a sin-sick and sin-darkened environment, in the process of being sanctified, weaned off a sin-indulgent and self-centred lifestyle. The pathway of our life is therefore hindered and bogged down. Knowing God's all-embracing and affirming love may not change our outward circumstances. But it can enable us inwardly to 'sing for joy and be glad all our days' (v. 14). These lessons about time awareness, increasing consciousness of God in everything all the time, can lead us to that place of singing. They will enable us to 'gain a heart' of true wisdom.

FOR REFLECTION

1. What might be some practical reasons why the issue of time management is applicable to us personally?

2. Why can it be hard to face up to the fact that we are unlikely to accomplish all the ambitions that we have? In what ways can the words of Jesus, 'I have come that they may have life, and have it to the full' (John 10:10), help us to face this inability to accomplish our aims?

3. What are some of the factors that might determine, as we assess demands on our time, which activities we should pursue and those we should leave or delay?

4. Although we need to accept ultimate responsibility for our use of time and energy, what are the advantages in involving other people in helping assess priorities? And who should we ask?

5. What practical tools are available in helping keep track of appointments, deadlines and events? What are the advantages and disadvantages of each one?

6. How can a sense of God being involved in all that we undertake bring us encouragement?

7

GOD: BEYOND THAT FULL STOP

The eternal God is your refuge, and underneath are the everlasting
arms.
(Deuteronomy 33:27)

The *Railway Children* is a film with a genuine 'feel-good' factor. Set in Edwardian England it tells the story of a well-to-do family deprived of husband and father following police arrest. With the head of the household in prison accused of financial irregularities, the mother has to 'downsize'. So she takes herself and her children to live in a rundown country cottage in the north of England.

A nearby railway is the setting for their subsequent adventures... and the climax to the film. News reaches the children that their father has eventually been released and is due to arrive at the local station. The teenage daughter goes to stand at the end of the platform as the train puffs in... and then leaves without any sign of him. The atmosphere of that northern location in late autumn is used to good effect. As the girl remains forlornly watching the steam train disappear, she strains her eyes through the mist, steam and smog. Suddenly, within the haze, she sees the faint outline of a man. The lifting smoke reveals this to be her daddy who has been there all the time... and they unite in a loving embrace (while the film audience are moved to tears!).

THE FULL STOPS OF TIME...

There are many characters in the Bible whose lives seemed to be over. The 'train' of opportunity and change would seem to have 'steamed' away from their 'platform' many years previously. The world would have viewed such people as Abraham, Joseph and Moses as having passed the point of no return.

Abraham was too old to have a family, so essential to life and culture in his day. He had obeyed God's call to leave his homeland, society and loved ones to head towards an unknown destination. Although amassing large herds of livestock, he complained to God that this wealth would eventually be inherited by his chief steward. This was on account of him having no heir (see Genesis 15:1–3). There was no likelihood of change since his wife was now too old to have children; Abraham himself was nearing the time when fathering a family would no longer be possible.

A full stop also existed in Joseph's life. He was serving an indefinite prison sentence. Sold as a slave by his jealous brothers who sought to put an end to Joseph's 'dreams' regarding being in a place of power, he had ended up in Egypt. Falsely accused of rape, that prison environment appeared to be the end of the road.

Forced exile was the plight that Moses was experiencing. Raised in the surroundings of Pharaoh's court, he had been earmarked for high office. But he had had to flee as an outlaw for an act of murder, protecting one of his Hebrew countrymen. Now in the desert, although at liberty, he was physically and figuratively nowhere, simply caring for sheep.

...AND OUR OWN

However, God had not left any of these men. He saw their situations very differently from other people. For them, and for those observing, time looked like it had become a 'full stop'. There was nothing outside their present situation. But God saw beyond those scenarios. There was more to come, even though it was not obvious... even though time might now look like a 'question mark'. The problem is, of course, that we may well identify with these situations. While our circumstances are likely to be very different, we could fear that our 'sell-by' date has passed and our place in God's plans no longer exists. There may be times when we also feel that He is far away, unconcerned, or that He has 'lost the plot'. Each of those men mentioned above could have ticked such boxes. God, however, still had time for them... and He still has time for you and me.

REMOVING THE FULL STOP: CORE BELIEF...

But what were the elements that meant that these men, and so many other people described in the Bible, could actually experience change? What removed the full stops of their time, and how can this also relate to ourselves? There are three particular emerging attitudes which provided the essential basis for change. The first of these was a core belief in God and experiencing Him in a personal way. Abraham clearly exhibited such a belief... even if it was expressed in a negative way! When he raised that complaint about his childless plight, he was directing it towards God, not his wife, his work colleagues, nor his Facebook page. The psalmist took a similar route:

> I cry aloud to the LORD;
> I lift up my voice to the LORD for mercy.
> I pour out my complaint before him;
> before him I tell my trouble.
>
> (Psalm 142:1–2, NIV1984)

In the account of Joseph there is a lack of any mention of God until the young man is in Egypt, serving as a slave in the household of Potiphar, one of Pharaoh's officials. While Joseph is in the role of being in overall charge, Potiphar's wife attempts to seduce him. His refusal reveals his deep belief: 'How then could I do such a wicked thing and sin against God?' (Genesis 39:9). In the case of Moses his act of murder had been the outworking of something much deeper than even trying to redress an injustice. He had a belief in God and the specialness of His people, the Hebrews. 'By faith Moses, when he had grown up, refused to be known as the son of Pharaoh's daughter. He chose to be ill-treated along with the people of God rather than to enjoy the fleeting pleasures of sin' (Hebrews 11:24–25). While there is no record of either Joseph or Moses having dialogue with God in these opening stages, Abraham's troubled comments show that being 'real' with God can actually reinforce our relationship with Him. Raising the details about those full stops of our time is a step towards seeing them removed.

...TENACITY...

However, there is a further step that we need to take. Again it's seen in the lives of these three men. They each had an attitude of tenacity. Somewhere and somehow they held on to what God had previously spoken (through message or action) to them. This may have meant hanging on by their fingernails, but they didn't let God's promises slip away. At the outset Abraham had received a declaration from God:

> I will make you into a great nation
> and I will bless you;
> I will make your name great,
> and you will be a blessing.
> I will bless those who bless you,
> and whoever curses you I will curse ....
>
> (Genesis 12:2–3)

Abraham had this promise subsequently underlined. A covenant act was performed, with God again speaking: 'To your descendants I give this land, from the Wadi of Egypt to the great river, the Euphrates – the land of the Kenites, Kenizzites, Kadmonites, Hittites, Perizzites, Rephaites, Amorites, Canaanites, Girgashites and Jebusites' (Genesis 15:18–21).

Joseph's dreams – God's revelation to him of the purposes mapped out ahead – had clearly not been discarded. The evidence comes from Joseph's attitude towards Pharaoh's cupbearer and baker who were thrown into prison with him. When they were given dreams which caused them to look dejected the following day, Joseph's response was to ask the question: 'Do not interpretations belong to God? Tell me your dreams' (Genesis 40:8). His positive approach and subsequent interpretation indicated a belief in God's authorship and power to bring dreams to life, even though his own were yet to be birthed.

In the case of Moses, the Hand of God was clearly on his life from the very beginning. His parents had seen, by faith, that their baby was 'no ordinary child, and they were not afraid of the king's edict' (Hebrews 11:23). As a consequence he had been famously hidden in the reeds alongside the River Nile, placed in a watertight papyrus basket. A careful lookout was kept by his sister. This meant that when Pharaoh's own daughter found the baby and felt sorry for him, Miriam was on hand to volunteer her mother to nurse him.

God still 'speaks' to us, individually and personally, through words and actions. These bring us affirmation and a sense of value, also giving direction and purpose, confirming that His timing does not have full stops. Jesus said: 'My sheep listen to my voice; I know them and they follow me.' 'The words I have spoken to you – they are full of the Spirit and life' (John 10:27; 6:63).

"..His timing does not have full stops"

The amazing comment made to Eddie Stobart (founder of the road haulage company) and his wife, both committed Christians, at their wedding is an example of God speaking. A close Christian friend gave a speech at their reception drawing attention to the requirements of Proverbs 3:5–6 ('Trust in the LORD with all your heart ...') before saying that he felt that Eddie's name would become known throughout the land. At that time Eddie was simply an enterprising businessman operating in a corner of Cumberland. But subsequent events, which included the need to tenaciously trust God, resulted in the 'Stobart' name being advertised on the road network of the UK and beyond. This was a clear 'full stop' being removed! The New Testament writer summed this up when he encouraged the Hebrew Christians: 'We do not want you to become lazy, but to imitate those who through faith and patience inherit what has been promised' (Hebrews 6:12).

...AND TRUST

The last aspect regarding moving on from the full stops is the need to step out. This may well involve moving into the unknown – the 'question mark' as we may perceive it. Each of those biblical people discussed above had reached a point where they had to make such a move. Acting in that way led them to be listed in the great 'gallery' of faith-full men and women who somehow saw beyond their full stop.

But seeing in that way was not easy. Abraham, although he is described as the 'father of all who believe' (Romans 4:11) and although he set out for that unknown destination, faltered badly at times. He moved on from the Promised Land at a time of famine and, while in Egypt, tried to pass off his wife as his sister. This was out of fear rather than faith. Joseph had been thoughtlessly brash when revealing his dreams as a teenager. At the other end of the age spectrum, Moses was distinctly reluctant to respond to God. At a crucial point when God spoke to him out of a burning bush in the desert, he had almost 'rubber-stamped' that full stop in his life. But God was amazingly gracious and put in certain 'support mechanisms' to allay Moses' fears. He therefore took up the responsibility of being the leader of the Israelites to bring them, with God's help, out of slavery.

REFUGE

Each of these full stops in time may have changed to a question mark, but trusting in God and being conscious of His closeness was integral. Our own full stops may be very different. Perhaps they relate to finance, health, accommodation, relationship, parenting, employment or simply life itself. But none of these is outside of God's knowledge or control. The psalmist wrote: 'My times are in your hands' (Psalm 31:15). We may not know what the days ahead hold for us, but our Heavenly Father is with us. Perhaps, like the film The *Railway Children*, He is obscured by the mist and smoke, but we are not alone. The 'eternal God' is still our 'refuge, and underneath are the everlasting arms' (Deuteronomy 33:27).

GOD STOPPED TIME?

However, in looking at this aspect of God working beyond the full stops of our own time, we must not omit reference to a particularly serious question mark! This involves two occasions recorded in the Old Testament when God intervened, it seemed, to actually stop the passage of time. The question mark is raised because it's not made clear as to whether this simply affected the astronomical indicators or time itself.

Joshua's campaign of conquest of the Promised Land was the background to the first incident relating to time. The narrative describes his actions when the Israelites needed more daylight to complete a 'mopping up' operation:

> On the day the LORD gave the Amorites over to Israel, Joshua said to the LORD in the presence of Israel: 'Sun, stand still over Gibeon, and you, moon, over the Valley of Aijalon.' So the sun stood still, and the moon stopped, till the nation avenged itself on its enemies ... The sun stopped in the middle of the sky and delayed going down about a full day.
>
> (Joshua 10:12–13)

The second occasion took place many years later. King Hezekiah, the Godly ruler of Judah, was terminally ill. His response to the news from Isaiah, God's prophet, that it was time to put his house in order was to weep bitterly and ask God to remember his wholehearted devotion. As a consequence God sent a further message that 15 years would be added to his life. The confirmatory sign from God was that the shadow of the sun on the 'stairway of Ahaz' would go back – not forward – by ten steps (Isaiah 38).

It's been claimed that the North American Space Agency (NASA) discovered discrepancies when programming their space flights because of unaccountable inaccuracies in dates and time. These were put down to those biblical accounts. Although NASA's alleged problems may be an 'urban myth', the scriptural narrative again alerts us to the fact that God works outside of our concept of 'time' and is not controlled by it. With Him 'a day is like a thousand years, and a thousand years are like a day' (2 Peter 3:8).

A final aspect in seeing God at work beyond that full stop – one that is possibly more comprehensible – is His ability to seemingly speed up activities and events within the constraints of time. When King Hezekiah was re-establishing temple worship, evidence of turning back to God, it was recorded: 'Hezekiah and all the people rejoiced at what God had brought about for His people, because it was done so quickly" (2 Chronicles 29:36). The prophecy of Amos also points to God's ability to 'up the pace'. '"The days are coming," declares the LORD, "when the reaper will be overtaken by the ploughman and the planter by the one treading grapes."' (Amos 9:13)

A verse from another minor prophet in the Old Testament also speaks of God's ability to (somehow) 'make up' what had previously seemed lost in time past. "I will repay you for the years the locust has eaten" ("I will restore to you the years that the locust has eaten" KJV; Joel 2:25) My dad, having had to work in an office since leaving school, felt God underline this verse for him when having an opportunity to move into teaching late in life.

GOD'S EVERLASTING ARMS

Ultimately for ourselves, of course, the time will come when we pass on from this life. As the apostle Paul described it: 'The perishable must clothe itself with the imperishable, and the mortal with immortality' (1 Corinthians 15:53). All the full stops and question marks of time will then be removed... but God's everlasting arms will remain underneath us.

FOR REFLECTION

1. In what areas of your life do you feel that there is a 'full stop' and that time for anything to change is no longer present?

2. How can the truth of God's 'everlasting arms' being 'underneath' you give hope that God can bring change into your life?

3. What hope can also be derived from the fact that (somehow) God is able to 'speed up' events and circumstances in our lives?

4. What promises or aspirations from God do you hold which have not yet come into being? What assurance for our lives can be drawn from the psalmist's declaration: 'My times are in your hands?' whether or not we sense that we have such promises?

8

LAST-MINUTE-DOT-COM

Now the LORD was gracious to Sarah as he had said, and the LORD did for Sarah what he had promised. Sarah became pregnant and bore a son to Abraham in his old age, at the very time God had promised him.

(Genesis 21:1–2)

It's not just an internet holiday booking website. 'Last-minute-dot-com' is now a label identifying people who tend to leave things to the last possible moment... or even later. The scenarios in which such situations are worked out are endless. They can also be intriguing to witness, as was the case when I was browsing the shelves of a bookshop. The pleasure of this occasion was disturbed by overhearing one side of a conversation. But as I listened to the bookshop manager's attempt to help with a customer's phone enquiry, the inevitability of the outcome was obvious. The caller wanted some material for a course that he or she was starting. The manager was scouring the relevant shelves to locate the required books. Mobile phone in one hand, sorting through book covers with the other, nothing was found. This would not have been a problem in normal circumstances as the necessary litera-ture could easily be ordered. But there was one problem. This emerged as I listened to this side of the discussion. The material was needed for tomorrow evening. 'Last-minute-dot-com' had struck again! Given the distances involved and lateness of the hour, I guessed the response of the manager. No way could the books be available. My sympathetic comment, subsequently made to the manager, about people optimistically wanting things today – or even sooner – was met with a wry smile.

Sometimes the 'last minute' aspect can arise simply because of the pressure of circumstances, unforeseen events or unsurmountable obstacles. Unfortunately the schedules of departing trains, planes or buses are unlikely to take these into account. Neither do other people or situations. So the necessity to 'factor in' possible delays, hindrances or incidents needs to be understood. Time, of course, is the crucial element. It cannot be stretched, slowed down or altered in order to avoid the consequences of 'last-minute-dot-com' eventualities. A few seconds, or even less, can entirely alter a planned event.

THE ZONE

God, as we read in the Bible, sometimes seems to operate within that last-minute-dot-com zone. There are times when His clear intervention occurs at the last possible moment, if not after it. This is inevitably stressful for those of us who like to operate within clear margins of time. After all, if we take the effort and forethought to schedule, plan and do our 'homework', why shouldn't God cooperate and work things out in good time from His end? However, what we need to learn is that God works to a different agenda from our own. The date on the calendar may be getting closer, the hand on the clock edging nearer, the sun setting deeper on the horizon, all to our consternation. But God is likely to want other issues to be addressed rather than simply allowing our tasks to be neatly achieved within a set timeframe. He is more concerned about enhancing our relationship with Him, deepening our trust, and creating space for His purposes to be carried out. We don't always see those 'angles' on events. God is the Master when it comes to last-minute-dot-com!

INTERVENTION BEYOND THAT 'LAST MINUTE'

In the Old Testament, God's mastery in the context of last-minute-dot-com is particularly seen in the events surrounding Abraham. For both him and his wife, Sarah, the particular 'clock' that was 'ticking' was the biological one. There were childless, and not only were they subject to natural and cultural drives to change that situation, but they also had God's promise as a factor. God had told Abraham that he would have offspring whose descendants would be countless and a blessing to the whole world. When the time was reached in Sarah's life when she could not become a mother, she urged her husband to go down the 'surrogate' route. As a result, Abraham fathered a son through Hagar who was Sarah's Egyptian maidservant. Significant tension arose as a result. This was not the direction that God was intending to take.

So the clock kept ticking. It then reached a point where Abraham himself was no longer able to father an heir. Yet he somehow clung on to God's promise. There was no longer any point in looking at the calendar. Instead Abraham looked to God. 'Without weakening in his faith, he faced the fact that this body was as good as dead – since he was about a hundred years old – and that Sarah's womb was also dead' (Romans 4:19). This was now beyond that 'last minute' deadline.

But God stepped into the situation in a clear way:

> Now the LORD was gracious to Sarah as he had said, and the
> LORD did for Sarah what he had promised. Sarah became
> pregnant and bore a son to Abraham in his old age, at the
> very time God had promised him. Abraham gave the name
> Isaac to the son Sarah bore him.
>
> (Genesis 21:1–5)

'Isaac' means 'He laughs'. Those years of waiting had not been
easy. But laughter was now the response of those parents to
God's provision that had been made well outside the last-minute-
dot-com timeframe. Somehow, during those many days, faith had
been enhanced despite the absence of any tangible fulfilment of
God's promise.

TOO LATE!

At the other end of the spectrum, Jairus in the New Testament
experienced the intervention of God when life had ended. His
daughter had been sick and was now recognised as being in her
last days. That's why her father, an official in a Jewish synagogue,
had come to Jesus. His plea had been a desperate one: 'My little
daughter is dying. Please come and put your hands on her so that
she will be healed and live' (Mark 5:23). No doubt the adage,
'Where there's life there's hope', was in his mind.

But there was a delay. A woman who was suffering from
uncontrolled bleeding was among the large crowd that then
followed Jesus. She reasoned that by simply touching Jesus' cloak
she would be healed. This, she thought, could be achieved
without her stigma being publicly known, since her condition
was one which rendered her ceremonially unclean. It had caused

her to spend all that she possessed on medical attention and suffer a great deal in the process. However, she had not been cured. But touching Jesus' cloak brought the healing that she sought. This was not in the obscure

> "..He was master over time.."

way that she desired. Jesus recognised that healing power had 'gone out from him' (Mark 5:30). She had to disclose her identity, telling Him the whole truth in front of that crowd.

However, even as Jesus spoke to the woman, bringing her words of assurance and inner healing for the deep wounds that she had suffered, other people appeared on the scene. Men came from Jairus' home with the terrible message: 'Your daughter is dead.' For them, and for Jairus himself, that was the end. It was now too late. There was no time even for last-minute-dot-com to come into operation. Hence their rhetorical question: 'Why bother the teacher anymore?' (Mark 5:35). But Jesus' response brought a different perspective. His encouragement indicated that He was master over time as well as physical life. Jesus told the synagogue ruler: 'Don't be afraid; just believe' (Mark 5:36). Jesus had to take action to eject the official mourners from the home before taking the girl's hand and speaking life into her body. 'Immediately the girl stood up and began to walk around.' The Gospel account adds an interesting element regarding time. The girl was 12 years old, this being the same period of time during which the sick woman had been suffering her condition (see Mark 5:25, 42).

OUTSIDE OUR TIMEFRAME

This was one of only three recorded occasions when Jesus brought a dead person back to life. Lazarus' raising from the dead was another one where Jesus had operated 'off the scale' as far as last-minute-dot-com was concerned. In that case He had deliberately delayed His arrival at Lazarus' home in Bethany by four days. By that time His friend was dead and in the tomb. Both sets of delays seemed to have spelt disaster at the time, but actually proved an opportunity for God's great power to be revealed, well outside that 'dot-com' possibility. Our own hopes and dreams may have been lost because the time for them to come about has gone. But, even outside our timeframe, Jesus is able to intervene and bring resurrection as we look to Him.

IN PRISON

In the case of Peter, the apostle, events did not quite 'reach the wire', but they got very close. He had been arrested by command of King Herod and put in prison. It was planned that he would be brought out for public trial after the feast of Passover. The outcome of this pending court appearance was not in doubt. He would suffer the same fate as that which befell James, his fellow disciple, and be executed. But there was one factor that the authorities did not take into account: 'So Peter was kept in prison, but the church was earnestly praying to God for him' (Acts 12:5). The last-minute-dot-com aspect was described in the following verses: 'The night before Herod was to bring him to trial, Peter was sleeping between two soldiers, bound with two chains, and sentries stood guard at the entrance. Suddenly an angel of the Lord appeared, and a light shone in the cell' (Acts 12:6–7). The angel woke Peter up and, with his chains falling off, together with the prison gates opening up before them, Peter was freed. The apostle then went to the house of Mary, the mother of John, where the Christians were meeting to pray for his release. Their reaction to seeing him – they are described as 'astonished' (v. 16) – perhaps reflected disbelief in the face of this impossible last-minute miracle.

HOT CROSS BUNS

God's ability to intervene at the last possible moment has not been restricted to the early Church. His operations in that 'dot-com' zone have continued! Fast forward many centuries and miles to the east of London and a more recent miracle involving God at the last moment. This was related in the account of Mill Grove, the home set up in the early 1900s by Herbert White on the outskirts of the city to care for orphaned children. Only this time it involved the timely provision of food.

> One of the things Linda and Anne [two children in the home] remember that really helped them to keep going was the incident involving hot cross buns at Easter time one year. Money was scarce and treats were therefore rare between [the First and Second World] wars, so it was with great excitement that the children and staff looked forward to Good Friday morning with the prospect of hot cross buns for breakfast.

Herbert was a Christian, believing that God had directed him to set up this home and that He would provide the necessary finance and supplies. However, on this occasion there was no sign of any buns being provided as in previous years.

The account continued:

> Breakfast was just finishing and the time for prayers had come. Herbert was the last to pray. To all the family's surprise he ended by thanking God for the hot cross buns. It was faith pure and simple. But had it been misplaced?

The family muttered their 'Amens', some with a notable lack of conviction. The children in the Home might never know the whole story, but they knew that God had been asked and that the buns hadn't come. But just as they got up from the large table there was a squeal of brakes outside in the street. Herbert led his own family to the door to discover a van standing right outside. 'You Mr White?' the driver enquired. When he was assured that this was the case, he opened the back of the van with the words,'Ot cross buns for you.' It was as simple as that as far as he was concerned. All that remained was the carrying of the trays of buns into the house. That completed, he was off. No one knows who sent him, except that it was not from the usual source.

(Extract from Keith White, *A Place for Us*, Mill Grove, 1976; used with permission)

God had worked to provide what was needed at the last moment.

INSURANCE RENEWAL PREMIUM

Also on the east side of London, but in much more recent times, God's timely intervention was experienced in the area of finance. This was in respect of a small group of Christians undertaking work to supply foreign language literature for use by overseas churches, missionaries and individuals. The Gospel Printing Mission provided this evangelism and discipling material without cost. They trusted God to bring the resources to enable all the processes to be undertaken, together with postage for sending out the leaflets and booklets. On one particular Saturday morning the team had met for prayer. The necessary insurance renewal premium covering the Mission's equipment was due to be paid, at the end of the next week. But there were insufficient funds in the bank account to pay it. Prayer was therefore made to God for Him to supply the needed finance. By the end of that next week, after a period of some months during which only small donations had been received, the larger amounts required to make payment of this premium had arrived through the post.

God's awareness of time, as affecting ourselves, and His power over it is more prominent in these areas of last-minute-dot-com. The worship song speaking about time being in His hands is particularly evident in the scenarios described in this chapter. But it can also be experienced in our own circumstances: with God it's never too late! This is a motivation for us to pray, trust and wait... but not an excuse for us to find ourselves labelled in that 'dot-com' category!

FOR REFLECTION

1. Why is it probably wise to ensure that we don't leave things to the last minute when it's within our power to act sooner?

2. What lessons can we learn from the accounts of Abraham and Jairus in terms of trusting God even when the time for things to change may seem to have irrevocably passed?

3. The Bible commentator, Matthew Henry, wrote that God's delays are not His denials. What do you feel our attitude should be when we are experiencing delay?

4. Think about situations and people about whom you may have been praying and for which no visible answers have yet been received. How do you feel about things not yet having changed in the light of what you have just read? What do you feel that your respond should now be?

9

TAKING A BREAK

Then, because so many people were coming and going that they did not even have a chance to eat, he [Jesus] said to them, 'Come with me by yourselves to a quiet place and get some rest.'
(Mark 6:31)

Some books about personal or spiritual growth aim for an element of climax or challenge with the closing chapter. This one does not come into that category! Indeed the focus in these pages of this Section One is entirely the opposite. We're looking at the value and opportunities to 'take time out', 'take a break', and 'wind down'.

The story is told of two Japanese farmers, father and son, on their way to the big city. The father was happy in making an unhurried journey, stopping at the numerous villages en route to trade produce, chat, rest and eat. However, the son was in a hurry. He wanted to reach the city quickly in order to be where he reckoned the real 'action' was taking place. An unaccountable but noticeable flash in the sky in that direction added impetus to his drive. But the older man had insisted on their relaxed progress. Eventually, after pausing at the last village, they came to a hill where the road led down to the mass of streets and buildings that marked their destination. However, as they reached the brow an astonishing sight met their eyes. The city was a collection of smouldering ruins with buildings and infrastructure totally devastated. Had their arrival taken place earlier, then father and son would have been among the casualties of Hiroshima's nuclear bomb blast. A frenetic and activity-dominated lifestyle does not accomplish all that might be envisaged.

PAUSING

The book of Proverbs states: 'It is not good to have zeal without knowledge, nor to be hasty and miss the way' (Proverbs 19:2, NIV1984). There are significant benefits in not being hasty, taking pauses during our journey of life. We are in danger of 'missing the way' if these are not taken. Unfortunately the target-driven, smartphone-focused, schedule-orientated, achievement-based, clock-watching pressures that now exist (in church as well as the world at large) are predominant.

While it is clearly wise and helpful to make plans and take responsibilities, whatever the sphere of life in which we live, such actions need to take into account this element of 'pausing'. There's a certain irony in Mark, the Gospel writer, recording the occasion when Jesus directed His disciples: 'Come with me by yourselves to a quiet place and get some rest.' This irony arises because, of all the Gospels, Mark's is the most action-packed. For instance, although the shortest of all the four Gospels, it contains almost as many accounts of Jesus' miracles as the others. Indeed this direction which Jesus issued was a prelude to the miracle of the feeding of the five thousand. But within these words that He spoke there are aspects which are helpful to us regarding this need to pause.

A POSSIBILITY...

First of all we see that Jesus' words present an invitation. While it may be an 'invitation that can't be refused', there is the indication that it's an offer rather than a demand. Jesus was pointing His disciples towards a specific possibility that lay ahead. He was not referring to the situation that they were leaving. This is important since they had no desire to be reminded of the obvious: 'Because so many people were coming and going ... they did not even have a chance to eat.' By issuing this invitation He was also saying that it was actually OK for them to leave, if only temporarily, the activity-filled and energy-draining moments with which they had been preoccupied. That's good news for the rest of us too! The disciples had been engaged in God-appointed tasks: 'The apostles gathered round Jesus and reported to him all they had done and taught' (Mark 6:30). Our own roles and responsibilities may not be quite so obviously 'spiritual' as those of the disciples. Yet as we follow Jesus they are likely to be the tasks which we need to undertake. So, receiving an invitation towards the possibility of space away from such pressures is just as valid for ourselves.

...A PERSON...

However, the invitation of Jesus was not for His disciples to spend time enjoying the benefits of a five-star hotel by a sun-kissed sandy beach, although that might have been welcomed! He qualified His call by adding the words: '... with me by yourselves.' Essentially it meant that no one else was to accompany them and that this separation was to enable them to spend time with Jesus. While God clearly speaks in the Bible of always being present with us, our awareness of that fact is often pushed away by pressing and immediate circumstances.

The psalmist had no doubt regarding the value of time spent focusing on the presence of God without distraction. He wrote:

> As the deer pants for streams of water,
>   so my soul pants for you, my God.
> My soul thirsts for God, for the living God.
> (Psalm 42:1–2)

> Yes, my soul, find rest in God;
>   my hope comes from him.
>   (Psalm 62:5)

The temple building epitomised this presence of God to which the psalmist looked. In that context he stated:

> How lovely is your dwelling-place,
>   LORD Almighty!
> My soul yearns, even faints,
>   for the courts of the LORD;
> my heart and my flesh cry out
>   for the living God …
> Better is one day in your courts
>   than a thousand elsewhere;
> I would rather be a doorkeeper in the house
>   of my God
> than dwell in the tents of the wicked.
>   (Psalm 84:1–2, 10)

The invitation that Jesus issued brought with it the opportunity of a 'one-to-one' with Him – an opportunity that's still open to each of us.

Alongside this invitation of Jesus is the Old Testament example of God Himself. The creation account recorded that,

By the seventh day God had finished the work he had been
doing; so on the seventh day he rested from all his work.
Then God blessed the seventh day and made it holy, because
on it he rested from all the work of creating that he had
done.

(Genesis 2:2)

This subsequently formed the basis of the fourth Commandment
by which space was provided for us to focus on God, not
work:

Remember the Sabbath day by keeping it holy ... On it you
shall not do any work, neither you, nor your son or daughter,
nor your male or female servant, nor your animals ... For
in six days the LORD made the heavens and the earth ... but
he rested on the seventh day.

(Exodus 20:8–11)

...A PLACE...

The psalmist's reference to God's 'dwelling-place' and Jesus'
invitation to a 'quiet place' point to a specific destination. This
has implications for ourselves. It can mean physically getting
away from a pressured environment in which we may be
continually bombarded with demands and expectations. While
this idea may cause us to think of needing to travel long distances
to 'get away from it all', involving a big chunk of time and cash,
this isn't necessarily the case. There are other options. My own
experience has been very down to earth and cost-effective! When
working in a demanding office regime in London, part of a high-
profile government department, I would often simply go out for
a walk at lunchtime. Even in the city there were oases of

tranquillity such as open green spaces and quiet side roads. So I would walk around these and aim to deliberately shut out the morning's events in order to try and focus on God for a few moments. Sitting on a park bench with a Bible to read was also helpful in that respect.

A friend of mine, also working in London, used to make it his practice to spend time inside a church, which was open to the public, while en route to his office. He had very heavy family and work responsibilities, but this opportunity to be in a place away from both was a means of briefly focusing on God.

"..time to.. think about God.."

Choosing alternative means of travelling around can also provide an option for spending time with God. Instead of driving a car, with all its requirements of concentration regarding traffic, using public transport might give us time to stop and think about God – even in a crowded Tube carriage! Again in that context of work, my own 'commute' provided opportunity to direct my thoughts in a more spiritually beneficial direction. Cycling on 'off road' paths facilitated such reflection. This was particularly the case when pedalling along a canal towpath which formed part of my journey. In the twilight of a winter afternoon the aroma of wood-burning stoves rising from the chimneys of moored barges created a very relaxing environment in which to push aside the events of the day.

'Digital detox' is another approach. Turning off, not logging on, and generally getting away from the technologies that blast us with information and messages may not be practical for lengthy periods. But taking such a break for a period of time might be feasible. Certainly, leaving mobile phones away from attention during church services ought to be possible... although it's observable that even taking those steps proves to be difficult for some. Moments of reflection on God need not be hard to find, even in a busy lifestyle.

...AND A PURPOSE

The account in Mark's Gospel included the reason that Jesus specified for the disciples' 'time out' session. It was to 'get some rest'. A similar meaning of the original Greek word for 'rest' is brought out in other parts of the New Testament. On one occasion Jesus spoke of the need to turn to Him: 'Take my yoke upon you ... for I am gentle and humble in heart, and you will find rest for your souls' (Matthew 11:29). The apostle Paul wrote of the particular support that he had received from named individuals:

> For they refreshed my spirit and yours also.
>
> (1 Corinthians 16:18)

> In addition to our own encouragement, we were especially delighted to see how happy Titus was, because his spirit has been refreshed by all of you.
>
> (2 Corinthians 7:13)

> Your love has given me great joy and encouragement, because you, brother, have refreshed the hearts of the Lord's people.
>
> (Philemon 7)

Paul clearly recognised and valued the opportunity to be 'refreshed' or rested. This is not only necessary in terms of physical and mental tiredness, but also (and more importantly) on account of our emotional and spiritual state.

However, these opportunities for rest and refreshment are in short supply in our technological and purpose-driven age. But God is not ignorant of the need that exists. He alone can give us this refreshment, as the psalmist underlines:

> He makes me lie down in green pastures,
>   he leads me beside quiet waters,
> he refreshes my soul.
>
>   (Psalm 23:2–3)

There may be many practical ways in which this can be experienced, depending upon our temperament. But it's always going to centre on God as being the source and sustainer of our lives at the deepest level.

> Truly my soul finds rest in God;
>   my salvation comes from him.
> Truly he is my rock and my salvation;
>   he is my fortress, I shall never be shaken.
> (Psalm 62:1–2)

Taking 'time out' with God means, like Elijah, hearing God speak. The 'gentle whisper' which the prophet experienced was distinct from the wind, earthquake and fire that preceded it. These latter phenomena perhaps typified the dynamic activity in which Elijah had been engaged up to that point. But now God had brought him to a place of aloneness, away from distraction, for that needed 'one-to-one'. This had not been an easy journey, involving a time element of 40 days and nights. But it got Elijah to the point where, having time out, God could fulfil the purpose of giving him a necessary change of perspective and renewed vision – factors which will also benefit us.

FULL CIRCLE

So we have almost come full circle. The seemingly inevitable march of time was our starting point. But instead of the 'full stop' which time seemed to present we have come to find that God intervenes. This comes in terms of experiencing His presence in our lives and being aware of the things that He wants to carry out. However, we have also seen that His work is accomplished both in the context of time and outside of it. This means that, as our relationship with Him is deepened, the time element of our lives changes to be more of a 'question mark'. Our knowledge and understanding of what God is doing – and when – is inevitably going to be limited. In the course of our journey we may raise many question marks of our own! But our trust is in God who is 'from everlasting to everlasting' (Psalm 90:2). We can have confidence that 'he who began a good work in you will carry it on to completion until the day of Christ Jesus' (Philippians 1:6) – however long it takes!

FOR REFLECTION

1. Why is it likely that we find it hard to take 'time out' in order to pause and reflect on God and our relationship with Him?

2. What perspective is brought by knowing that God actually invites us to 'take a break' for such reflection?

3. In what ways can we be more real in having a 'one-to-one' with God?

4. What geographical places feature in your routine that might present an opportunity to take time out with God?

5. List the different aspects of your life into which you feel, at this time, you need God to bring His encouragement, envisioning and refreshment. When can you best talk to Him about these aspects?

6. In what ways has time seemed to have been a full stop for you? How can your view of God help this change to being more of a question mark?

SECTION TWO

10

PROVOCATION: INTRODUCING ECCLESIASTES 3, 'A TIME TO...'

There is a time for everything ...
(Ecclesiastes 3:1)

The *Metro* morning newspaper available to commuters in London and other cities around the UK consistently parades hard-hitting headlines. They are designed to attract the attention of sleepy travellers on their way to work. But they also aim to provoke some kind of response, perhaps to engage readers to look more deeply at issues. From personal experience this latter approach doesn't always succeed so early in the day!

The book of Ecclesiastes was written by 'the Teacher' ('Preacher', KJV; 1:1). He stated that he was 'son of David, king of Jerusalem'. Although this strongly indicates that King Solomon was the human author, not all Bible commentators are convinced that this is the case. But although the writer's identity may be uncertain his style is unmistakable. It aims at being provocative. Rather like those headlines in a *Metro* newspaper, his opening words are designed to grab our attention: '"Meaningless! Meaningless!" says the Teacher' ('Vanity of vanities, saith the Preacher', KJV; 1:2).

'REINVENTING THE WHEEL'

Having caught our attention, the Teacher elaborates on this theme of everything being 'meaningless'. Examples from nature are included to show that this perspective is not limited to human activity. The workings of the natural world are also basically cyclical. It is within this list that the well-known saying appears: 'there is nothing new under the sun' (1:9). The more contemporary phrase, 'reinventing the wheel', conveys a similar idea. People may believe that their ideas are new and unique, but actually somewhere, and sometime previously, it's all been done before. The work environment is a good example of things 'coming round again'. In my own experience, employed in an office of a large government organisation, I have frequently witnessed newly appointed managers coming up with 'new' ideas to 'improve' and 'streamline' procedures. Those of us who'd been around for some time used to inwardly sigh and think, 'Here we go again.' The wheel having been reinvented, those self-same managers would then head off to another project, most likely leaving us to repair the damage that they had left behind!

But it's the opening question raised in Ecclesiastes that is poignant: 'What does man gain from all his labour at which he toils under the sun?' (1:3, NIV1984). Inspired by God, this is the first of several pointed questions and statements contained in the book. They are designed to detail the author's attempt to find purpose and meaning in life. This is very relevant to our own times. Individuals and society in this contemporary age are seriously questioning and closely examining the values and attitudes of previous generations. Reinventing the wheel is not an option which brings satisfaction. All of this has considerable ramifications not just in generating debate and dialogue, but for the very foundations of modern living. As a result our personal lives can be significantly impacted.

CLOSE TO THE MARK

So the issues raised and described in Ecclesiastes are both topical and demand answers. But they are also ones that we'd rather not face. They are too personal and close to the mark. Being told that specific aspects of our lives that we consider essential and integral are actually 'meaningless' is not a particularly positive tactic!

Yet being faced with provocative 'headlines' highlights the necessity of carefully thinking about our actions and attitudes. Even those of us who believe in having a close relationship with God are not exempt. We need to think about the reasoning behind what we do; our priorities can easily become misdirected and warped. The two opening chapters record the writer's attempts to find meaning and purpose in the key areas of education, enjoyment, enrichment and employment. Certainly the first and last of these would be held by Christians to be of value. But the 'Teacher's' conclusion? '… a chasing after the wind …This too is meaningless … a chasing after the wind' (1:17; 2:15; 2:26).

ANOTHER PERSPECTIVE

But God is not absent from the scenario that's presented in Ecclesiastes. Indeed the Teacher's aim is to refocus our attention and help us see another perspective – involving God in our lives. It is the absence of God that results in such 'meaningless' activity. Only an awareness of God can enable us to find order and purpose. Without Him there is only this 'chasing after the wind'.

So the author sets about showing this order and purpose by initially directing us to the different seasons and times of life... and to God who oversees them. The following chapters in this Section Two look at some of the aspects of this list of 'life events' described in Ecclesiastes 3:1–8. But it's important to notice that the Teacher is not throwing into these verses a series of random events plucked haphazardly out of his own life experiences. Instead he aims to provide a set of firm footholds on which we may all tread, in contrast to the almost desperate scenarios that precede them.

TIMES AND SEASONS

The first thing to note about the list in Ecclesiastes 3 is that the different phases of life are relevant to all of us. Whatever our age, social grouping, education, upbringing, skills or environment, they will all be experiences through which we will need to pass, sooner or later in time.

Secondly, those times and seasons may seem to be uncontrolled and indiscriminate. But the words that conclude this section put them in a different light: 'He has made everything beautiful in its time. He has also set eternity in the human heart' (3:11). God is described as being involved in what's taking place. This involvement is not always obvious. Nor are the reasons for these experiences always very clear. But knowing that we are not subject to capricious or malicious unknown forces can bring a measure of confidence. As the psalmist reminds us: 'My times are in your hands; deliver me from the hands of my enemies, from those who pursue me' (Psalm 31:15). We had previously noted that time may be an element of life completely outside of our control, but not outside of God's.

Thirdly, this group of verses presents times and seasons which are identifiable. Our problem is that the sheer pace of life, and the pressures that it brings, prevent us from taking stock. We have schedules and appointments, 'to do' lists and 'must do' lists, goals to achieve and ambitions to fulfil... preferably done today or sooner! We are constantly being driven to look ahead. But God wants us to slow down and pause. Perhaps this is why so much of what we end up doing seems so 'meaningless'. There's too much 'chasing.' In contrast the psalmist was inspired to write: 'Be still, and know that I am God' (Psalm 46:10).

VALUE

Next, these different times and seasons point to God working through them to deepen our relationship with Him, and bring spiritual maturity. A sense of frustration and aimlessness can easily arise when we face difficult circumstances. We may find our own set of provocative questions coming to mind: why are things not happening in the way and in the timeframe that I need? Where is God in what's going on? Will things ever change? But somehow, through the times outlined in these verses, God is able and wanting to shape and transform us. This was the experience of Jesus. He did not get 'fast-tracked' – neither will we! Thirty years of preparation preceded three years of ministry. Even then Jesus was taking one step at a time. His first miracle took place after He had stated to His mother: 'My time has not yet come' (John 2:4, NIV1984). The miracle of turning water into wine was not witnessed – the day for a public demonstration of His Spirit-anointed power had not arrived.

Jesus knew the importance of timing and the value of 'now'. His life included 'times' of beginnings and endings, tearing down and building, weeping and laughing, being silent and speaking. Each had value in seeing the Kingdom of God being enlarged on this earth. So our experiences, harsh as they may seem, can somehow and somewhere have value.

Lastly, these experiences will not last. It's recorded that God 'changes times and seasons' (Daniel 2:21). The backdrop to all events with which we have to contend is that eternity lies before us. God has 'set eternity in the hearts of men'. Our dim perception that this life is not the end brings an awareness that 'this, too, shall pass'.

REMEMBER...

The theme of 'time' is not restricted to those earlier verses in Ecclesiastes. There is a thread running through all the chapters. The last one brings specific encouragement. We are instructed by the Teacher: 'Remember your Creator in the days of your youth, before the days of trouble come and the years approach when you will say, "I find no pleasure in them"' (12:1). We are also to 'remember him – before the silver cord is severed, and the golden bowl is broken' (12:6). This is referring to our days on this earth coming to an end. In considering each of the seven couplets contained in Ecclesiastes 3 we should have the aim of 'remembering'. We need to focus on God being ever-present in the events that are described, whatever the time or season.

FOR REFLECTION

1. Why would someone, not taking God into account, be likely to conclude that events in life are ultimately 'meaningless'?

2. Why are the life events listed in Ecclesiastes 3:2–8 likely to be experienced by all of us whatever our background or upbringing?

3. How can an understanding of God being present in all of our 'ups and downs' help to provide us with a firmer footing in our lives?

4. How can slowing down (at least occasionally!) help us to be more aware of what we are actually going through, and more aware of God's perspective in such circumstances?

For a more detailed study of Ecclesiastes, see Christopher Brearley, *Is Life Worth Living?* (Zaccmedia, 2016).

11

BEGINNINGS
AND ENDINGS

... a time to be born and a time to die, a time to plant and a time to
uproot ...
(Ecclesiastes 3:2)

Obituaries seem to hold a certain fascination. A compilation in book form of recent notable or unusual obituaries has been regularly published by a national UK newspaper. That same publication also features the 'hatches' and 'matches' which are seemingly scanned regularly by readers. So it's not surprising that the Teacher in Ecclesiastes commences his series of statements with one that focuses on beginnings and endings – experiences that involve all of us whether we like it or not.

GOD'S INVOLVEMENT
This verse is a reminder of our finite existence in this world. It also points to our inability to have any input into these essential moments. We have no 'say' regarding our birth. Our own actions may contribute to the end of our journey on earth but ultimately it's out of our hands. The unpredictability of life is sometimes very evident – healthy young sports-crazy people suddenly collapse while inactive heavy smokers and drinkers

live to old age. From our perspective, who can tell what a day will bring?

However limited our influence in these and other life-shaping events, the Teacher wants to underline that they are not random. Again referring to the verse that follows this section, there is the reminder of God's involvement: 'He has made everything beautiful in its time.' Certainly God intervened in a very clear way in respect of the birth of Samson. While his subsequent interaction with Delilah has achieved a degree of notoriety, the fact that his mother had actually been childless and unable to give birth is not so well known. A whole chapter of the book of Judges (13) describes the intervention of God, through 'the angel of the LORD', with Manoah and his wife in which God stated that, in time, they would be parents of a son who was to be brought up as 'dedicated to God'.

NO ACCIDENT

The psalmist summed up God's involvement, convinced that the time of his birth was no accident:

> For you created my inmost being;
>   you knit me together in my mother's womb …
> all the days ordained from me were written
>   in your book
> before one of them came to be.
>
> (Psalm 139:13, 16)

Whatever the outward circumstances of our arrival on earth, neither our birth, nor its timing, has been an accident. The Bible clearly points to God's involvement in both aspects.

GATHERED TO YOUR PEOPLE

But those verses from Psalm 139 also indicate an ending. What is God's involvement in that part of life? Again we can pick up accounts in the Bible where specific details are recorded. Moses was the great leader of the Israelites. He'd been instrumental in enabling the people of God to escape from Egypt. But God told him that he would not himself enter the Promised Land. So when Canaan appeared on the horizon God spoke to Moses:

> Go up into the Abarim Range to Mount Nebo in Moab, opposite Jericho, and view Canaan, the land I am giving the Israelites as their own possession. There on the mountain that you have climbed you will die and be gathered to your people …

(Deuteronomy 32:49–50)

So Moses' time on this earth was ended.

But in an age where medical science now seems to have a lot of answers, God also intervenes to change anticipated 'endings'. A lady whom I met when visiting a local retirement home told me of her experience regarding her terminally ill daughter. The medical professionals had put her on a life-support system, advising that this would have to be switched off. But the mother, now the only one believing that God would restore her child, hung on to the words of Jesus, 'Don't be afraid; just believe.' She went to visit her daughter at that time who, unexpectedly, shared that she had sensed the presence of Jesus by her bed. It was at that point that her health started to improve, and she subsequently staged a full but medically unexpected recovery. In matters concerning both birth and death, we need to remember that God has the final word!

BIRTHING

But endings can also make way for beginnings. The first recorded words of God to Joshua, leader of the Israelites, spoke of both death and life: 'Moses my servant is dead. Now then, you and all these people, get ready to cross the River Jordan' (Joshua 1:2). The death of Moses was the necessary stepping stone for birthing. It enabled the dream of the Israelites in entering the Promised Land to be realised. While it was a time of grieving and loss, it was to give way to practical preparation for something new and wonderful. It showed that God can use even the event of death as a means of bringing life.

HOPES AND DREAMS

But beginnings and endings can arise in other ways, not just with reference to physical life. As people we have dreams, hopes and ambitions. These may be 'birthed' in many and varied circumstances, sometimes in very unpromising environments. There may also be a long 'gestation' period. Winston Churchill was a Member of Parliament for almost 40 years and his aim of being Prime Minister of Great Britain appeared to be unfulfilled. But in most unlikely circumstances in 1940 he was appointed to that post.

But some dreams also die. King David aspired to oversee the construction of a massive temple of worship to God. But that dream did not materialise. God told him through the prophet Nathan that it would be his son (Solomon) who would be given that task. David had to be content simply to make the preparation for the building.

Our own dreams are likely to be on a smaller scale than David's. But their loss can be just as devastating. This was my experience having trained to be a school teacher and finding that the demands were overwhelming and I could not continue. However, God then opened a door to alternative employment that I had not envisaged. But what I found difficult was reconciling my perceived sense of calling with what actually happened. The dream may have died, but a 'post-mortem' of self-examination followed! This was compounded by the belief that Christians don't 'fail'. These feelings and confusion were gradually dispelled through assurance that

God had not 'written me off'. The 'birth' and 'death' of dreams can arise in many other areas, involving much heartache.

PLANTING

But this opening part of the couplet in Ecclesiastes 3 needs to be put alongside the second part: '... a time to plant and a time to uproot'. These words indicate our specific involvement in beginnings and endings. In contrast to birth and death, an element of our own control and responsibility is now suggested. God, it could be said, does His 'bit', but we have a contribution to make. 'Planting', as in the realm of agriculture, projects the idea of specific investment of time, effort and resources.

This is not a casual or incidental activity. We need to be alert to the right time in 'planting' out in this spiritual sense. This was a factor when the vicar of a nearby church moved to another parish and the congregation that he left needed support. Although, in time, a replacement was appointed, there was an 'interregnum' to be negotiated. As the church in which I was involved had already been providing support for this small congregation it was clear that more was needed. So for several months, and into the early stages of the new appointment, a group of us were 'planted out' to provide help until it was appropriate to 'uproot' ourselves.

POSITIVE STEPS

So it may be necessary to take positive steps to uproot. My kitchen garden provided a lesson in this respect! Growing runner beans is fairly straightforward. But as I found too late, the resultant crop had to be harvested promptly. Failure to 'uproot' in terms of picking those beans at the right time resulted in a very 'stringy' unpleasant taste!

However, the minor issues of growing vegetables cannot be compared with major upheavals in life. Jacob in the Old Testament had to go through that experience several times. The first involved him contriving to take away his twin brother's birthright and blessing. Both of these were of massive cultural and spiritual importance. So the reaction of his brother Esau in threatening his life was not surprising. As a consequence Jacob had to leave home… quickly. The timing of this uprooting was crucial to survival. Many years later he had to uproot again. This time it was in order to move to Egypt where his son, Joseph, was effectively Prime Minister. This was a consequence of some amazing interventions by God. But it meant that food supplies were available to him and his family at a time of widespread famine. Jacob had been reticent to uproot in this way. It took God's direct intervention by way of a vision to reassure him that this was OK (Genesis 46:1–4).

In a world of upheaval and uncertainty, when timing is crucial in these aspects of life – birth, death, planting and uprooting – the presence and promises of God are a 'constant' to bring us the same reassurance that Jacob received.

FOR REFLECTION

1. In what ways can we find affirmation in knowing that God has orchestrated the event and timing of our birth?

2. How can awareness of our limited time on this earth shape our thinking?

3. What factors should we take into account when deciding whether it's time to invest our energies and resources in a particular direction?

4. What factors should be taken into account in deciding if it's time to move from a particular commitment?

12

INTERVENTION

... a time to kill and a time to heal, a time to tear down and a time to build ...
(Ecclesiastes 3:3)

James Bond, the fictional secret service operative, has starred in many popular films. His calm, typically British, resourceful approach in the face of impossible odds has made his character somewhat iconic. But behind the facade of being laid-back is a steely resolve. He is, after all, Her Majesty's secret agent 007, 'licensed to kill'.

Almost from the outset the Bible reveals accounts of violence and death. Unlike '007' these are fact, not fiction. In addition, when we come to Ecclesiastes 3 in which we read that there is a 'time to kill', it is not describing something about which God is a passive or powerless observer. The Teacher stated that God 'has made everything beautiful in its time'. In some way God's intervention in this spiritually darkened world means involvement in this issue.

Clearly we are treading on serious ground. As people affected by sin we have limited understanding of God's ways. But that should not stop us from trying to determine what this verse means. Firstly it should be noted that this word, 'kill', is not the same word in Hebrew as 'murder'. It is the latter that is prohibited in the sixth Commandment (Exodus 20:13). Implicit in the word 'murder' is the concept of a criminal, malicious and personally motivated deed, undertaken out of a spirit of revenge or to seek advantage. Those aspects are not specifically tied up in the word 'kill'. But secondly 'kill' is not describing an event resulting from an accident, the result of neglect, or a freak unforeseen event. Implicit in Ecclesiastes is a definite act. Thirdly the context suggests an action that, in some way, is actually mandated by God. He is the One to whom Abraham voiced the rhetorical question: 'Will not the Judge of all the earth do right?' (Genesis 18:25). This was when God announced the imminent destruction of Sodom and Gomorrah. We need to be aware that God's actions always reflect His holiness and righteousness.

'LICENSED TO KILL'

There were occasions when God oversaw a killing. When David, as a youth, confronted Goliath, the enemy warrior, he declared: 'This day the Lord will deliver you into my hands, and I'll strike you down and cut off your head' (1 Samuel 17:46). He was in no doubt that God had 'licensed' him to carry out this act. Added to that declaration was the statement of faith going beyond Goliath's imminent death: 'This very day I will give the carcasses of the Philistine army to the birds ... and the whole world will know that there is a God in Israel ... the battle is the Lord's, and he will give all of you into our hands' (1 Samuel 17:46–47). The Philistine forces facing the army of Israel were threatening them with annihilation. Goliath typified the overwhelming power of spiritual evil. So God's authorisation was showing His intention to deal thoroughly with the wickedness represented by this giant, as had previously been the case with Israel's enemies at the time of the judges.

GOD'S MERCY

A common factor in such God-mandated acts included confronting the wickedness and evil and totally exterminating it. The act of killing was, as best as we can understand it, showing the horror and loathsomeness of sin. But something else also surfaced. When Jonah was directed to bring God's message of judgement and destruction upon the inhabitants of Nineveh there was an unforeseen outcome. The king of Nineveh led his people to repent of their 'evil ways'. To Jonah's chagrin God did not 'bring on them the destruction he had threatened' (see Jonah 3:7–10). There may have been a 'time to kill' in respect of this people-group, but because of their response this was deferred, as history records, to a later generation.

SORT THINGS OUT

But the apostle Paul brings another 'angle' in respect of there being a 'time to kill'. He directs us to kill ('put to death') 'the misdeeds of the body' (Romans 8:13). This is repeated when writing to the Christians in Colosse: 'Put to death, therefore, whatever belongs to your earthly nature: sexual immorality, impurity, lust, evil desires and greed, which is idolatry … You used to walk in these ways, in the life you once lived' (Colossians 3:5–7).

This was the same approach that Jesus had when teaching His disciples – sin was to be dealt with ruthlessly. He emphasised this:

> If your right eye causes you to stumble, gouge it out and throw it away ... And if your right hand causes you to stumble, cut it off and throw it away. It is better for you to lose one part of your body than for your whole body to go into hell.

> (Matthew 5:29–30)

Physical mutilation was not being advocated. These were pictures showing that a resolute approach was needed.

A TIME TO HEAL...

But if God had given a 'licence' in respect of ending life, the Bible also shows that He steps in to bring wholeness. This is not only in spiritual terms but also physical. The psalmist linked these two aspects of God's intervention: 'Praise the Lord, my soul, and forget not all his benefits – who forgives all your sins and heals all your diseases' (Psalm 103:2–3). The ministry of Jesus was launched on the basis of words from the prophet Isaiah specifying this healing and wholeness:

> The Spirit of the Lord is on me,
>   because he has anointed me
>   to proclaim good news to the poor.
> He has sent me to proclaim freedom for the
>   prisoners
>   and recovery of sight to the blind,
> to set the oppressed free,
>   to proclaim the year of the Lord's favour.

Jesus then added: 'Today this scripture is fulfilled in your hearing' (Luke 4:18–19, 21). The ensuing three years were a record of timely interventions to bring physical healing, spiritual release, restoration, miraculous provision and inner wholeness.

The early Church, empowered by the Holy Spirit, continued to experience the intervening power of God. An early account describes Peter and John 'going up to the temple at the time of prayer – at three in the afternoon' (Acts 3:1). At that point they encountered a crippled beggar and were used by God to bring him healing. It's been commented that as this beggar was carried to that location 'every day', it is possible that Jesus also saw him. But the time for that man's healing was not yet on God's 'calendar' until Peter and John were alerted to the fact that this was now God's 'moment'.

BREAK DOWN

In the second part of this couplet in Ecclesiastes 3 the Teacher states that there is also a time to 'tear down'. To us in the twenty-first century this may simply seem to describe an act of demolition. However, the original Hebrew word was initially translated in the King James Version as 'break down'. All of the Old Testament passages in which it was used were in the context of breaking down walls surrounding cities or vineyards. In those days this was a particularly serious matter. City walls were a primary form of defence and, alongside gates within those walls, a vital form of control. When surrounding vineyards, such walls similarly provided defence and prevented the theft of valuable crops by either human or animal trespassers. But city walls also served another purpose. They made a clear 'statement'. Not only was this with regard to marking a physical boundary; it also related to 'identity'. It was the tangible expression of the 'separateness' and 'specialness' of those dwelling within the walls compared to those outside.

Breaking down city walls not only rendered the inhabitants vulnerable but also opened up the probability of capture and deportation. Nehemiah, hearing about the destruction of Jerusalem's walls by the Babylonian superpower, was totally distraught. He knew that this represented the brokenness of God's people who had once found their identity and distinctiveness in being within Jerusalem instead of trusting in God. The time of brokenness was therefore a means of pointing people back to God.

...AND A TIME TO BUILD

So a 'time to tear down' then progresses to there being a 'time to build'. The many uses of this word, 'build', in the Old Testament include a large number relating to altars. These were constructed as a means of worship and sacrifice to God. Sometimes it was in gratitude for what He had done. At other times it was a way of acknowledging His greatness. It was also a tangible form of rededication to Him (Genesis 12:7–8; 13:8; 26:25; 35:7). Each occasion was one of identifying and responding to God's intervention.

The Bible shows us that God is always working in this world and in our lives. But we aren't always aware of this fact. So the times when God's intervention is clearly revealed are occasions – even those negative ones – that demand our attention and response by way of recommitment to Him.

FOR REFLECTION

1. Why do you think that the apostle Paul used
    drastic language in describing the need to
    deal with sin? What steps can we take in
    respect of sin and what might determine
    the 'time' when this should be done?

2. When praying about healing, why can
    the element of timing be important?

3. What aspects of our lives can constitute
    'walls' by which we find our identity and
    sense of worth? Why may there be times
    when God allows them to be 'battered'?

4. In what ways can we 'build' a sense of
    rededication to God? Why can it be
    helpful to clearly mark such times?

13

GOING
OVERBOARD

... a time to weep and a time to laugh, a time to mourn and a time to dance ...
(Ecclesiastes 3:4)

The lower levels of the English Football League feature soccer teams whose ability and consistency is lacking – with some teams it's more obvious than with others! But within their respective small bands of loyal supporters a whole roller-coaster of emotions can be felt in the 90 minutes of just one match. I know that because I've been there. Watching my local team, Leyton Orient, is often an emotionally draining experience.

It's surprising how such minor events can cause emotions to be generated... and 'go overboard'. Sport is only one of many ways in which this can arise. But when the writer of Ecclesiastes 3 stated that there were times when emotions would be suitably expressed he probably didn't have a football match in mind! However, he was aware that life events can give rise to deep passions coming to the surface. They also do not come out of the blue. Something may have happened, either a few moments previously or perhaps years ago. In addition they are not superficial or transitory experiences but can be powerful and resonating. So when a penalty is scored or a goal is awarded, the crowd's response is to roar, cheer and clap. This doesn't happen very often at the Orient matches! It's more likely to be a goal conceded, a misplaced pass or bad tackle that causes the home crowd to groan and throw their hands up in despair.

WEEPING...

This response of spectators to an abject display of sporting ability introduces us, appropriately, to the first of these emotions recorded by the Teacher. In the original Hebrew language of the Old Testament this word, 'weep', described an abundant and continual flow of tears. There were many times when it was used. Baby Moses' crying while hidden alone in the reeds of the River Nile made use of that word. It's not hard to imagine (even without the experience of parenting a baby) the continual and piercing sound it portrayed. The same word was used to describe the emotions of Hannah in her childless state, being provoked by her husband's other wife and mother of many children (1 Samuel 1:7–8).

In the case of both Moses and Hannah the sense of helplessness and hopelessness is evidenced by their response to situations. It was clearly very appropriate. Neither response went unheard. In Hannah's case she was weeping in the environs of the temple. Her tears were accompanied by unspoken prayer. It was this aspect that was noticed by the resident priest who accused her of drunkenness. Her reply described the attitude of her heart: 'I was pouring out my soul to the LORD ... I have been praying here out of my great anguish and grief' (1 Samuel 1:15).

...AND PRAYING

William Booth, founder of the Salvation Army, was contacted by officers working in the north of England on one occasion. They were asking to be moved to a different place. This was because despite much labour and prayer they had seen no result for their efforts. The General's reply was a telegram message containing just two words: 'Try tears.' The psalmist was inspired to bring hope when times of weeping arise from spiritual despair: 'He who goes out weeping, carrying seed to sow, will return with songs of joy, carrying sheaves with him' (Psalm 126:6, NIV1984).

LAUGHING

The words of Psalm 126 point us to the next emotion described in Ecclesiastes 3. Laughter can often arise when joy is experienced. But there weren't many occasions in the Old Testament when people were recorded as laughing. That's not because it was forbidden! The various feasts instituted through the Law of Moses were geared to bring joy and hope as God's people reflected on His goodness and provision. Nehemiah had specifically encouraged people in Jerusalem along those lines: 'Go and enjoy choice food and sweet drinks ... This day is holy to our Lord. Do not grieve, for the joy of the Lord is your strength' (Nehemiah 8:10).

The specific kind of laughter described by the Teacher, and its close linguistic equivalent, are confined to a few occasions. The most significant of these was when God appeared to Abraham to announce that the many years of waiting to have a family were now over. Overhearing these amazing words, Sarah's response was to laugh. The original Hebrew word does not elaborate on what kind of laugh this constituted. Was it ironic, sarcastic or derisory? The narrative simply reiterated the facts: she and Abraham were old and she was past childbearing. Although she had laughed 'to herself', the Lord had heard her and underlined His promise with a question of His own: 'Is anything too hard for the LORD?' (Genesis 18:14). Sarah then denied that she had laughed, perhaps indicative that her response had been negative. But He wasn't having any of it. 'Yes, you did laugh,' was His response.

SERIOUS STUFF

But 'laughter' remained on the agenda as far as Abraham and Sarah were concerned. When God's promise was fulfilled and Sarah gave birth to a son, Abraham named him 'Isaac'. This name meant 'He laughs', resulting in one of Israel's three great patriarchs bearing a name which would be a reminder throughout the nation's history that there is a 'time to laugh'. So actually, it can be a serious matter to 'laugh'! It needs to be the right response at the right moment, not just the result of hearing a good joke.

GRIEVING...

When it comes to mourning, that sense of deep emotions continues. It depicts the passionate beating of the breast and lamenting such as Abraham undertook when Sarah (his wife) died, and when Joseph with his brothers lost their aged father Jacob (Genesis 23:2; 50:10). Zechariah used this word to prophesy of a future time when the 'inhabitants of Jerusalem' will 'look on me [God], the one they have pierced, and they will ... grieve bitterly for him ... The land will mourn, each clan by itself' (12:10, 12).

In our present age the loss of friends and loved ones, especially close family, isn't always recognised as requiring a time of proper grieving. The sense of light-heartedness that is sometimes introduced into funerals can be counterproductive in preventing people from working through their grief. But God fully understands our feelings. He brought comfort and showed empathy to Mary and Martha, the grieving sisters of Lazarus their brother and friend of Jesus (John 11). God specifically stated though the prophet Isaiah that He would 'comfort all who mourn, and provide for those who grieve' (61:2–3). So God is clearly aware that there will be times when we need to mourn.

...AND DANCING

In contrast the 'dancing' which ends this couplet is not a formal, choreographed activity. It was a wholehearted skipping-like movement as performed by King David when the Ark of the Covenant was returned (1 Chronicles 15:29). The aspect of childlike, carefree abandonment is also inferred in the original Hebrew word. It was used by Job when replying to his friends at one point: 'They send forth their children as a flock; their little ones dance about' (21:11). So this is not the kind of movement likely to be displayed in the *Strictly Come Dancing* television competition! This is probably a relief to most of us – it means that we can engage in this response without fear of having a low score! Essentially we are responding to God, showing our delight in His love and provision.

EXPRESSED FEELINGS

Emotions are therefore clearly part of our God-given make-up. God Himself has emotions. Jesus, the Son of God, was described as weeping, having heaviness of spirit, but also being joyful (John 11:35; Matthew 26:38; Luke 10:21). So we should not be reticent in appropriate expression of feelings. There are times when this needs to be done whatever the reaction of others. We also need to remember that God is alongside whatever our emotional state. The psalmist states:

> The righteous cry out, and the LORD hears
> them;
> he delivers them from all their troubles.
> The LORD is close to the broken-hearted
> and saves those who are crushed in spirit.
> (Psalm 34:17–18)

The last aspect to remember is the part that we need to play in supporting others in bad times as well as good ones. This reflects the heart of God. 'Rejoice with those who rejoice; mourn with those who mourn' (Romans 12:15). We need to be sensitive not only to our own emotional responses but also to those of others... whatever the time.

FOR REFLECTION

1. How can weeping become a powerful driver in leading us to pray?

2. Why can the response of laughter when facing adversity suggest an attitude of faith and trust in God?

3. What has been your experience of having times of grieving and mourning? What factors helped you to move on from this response?

4. Why can dancing be liberating, especially in times of worship?

14

MAKING DECISIONS

... a time to scatter stones and a time to gather them, a time to embrace and a time to refrain ...

(Ecclesiastes 3:5)

It only required a cross to be entered into one of two boxes printed on the sheet of paper. Yet for many people that was the hardest choice they had had to make for a long time in terms of voting. Many factors made the national referendum in the UK regarding continued membership of the European Union a contentious event. But the situation which faced the 43 million potential voters was a unique one. Unlike a general election with many political candidates from which to choose, on this occasion there were only those two options. In addition parliamentary elections take place every five years. But this referendum was described as a once-in-a-lifetime event. These and other factors caused voters to struggle in placing their cross.

Of course there are many times when decisions are made without any problem. We are faced with choices every day. Whether they involve money, interacting with others, leisure activities or undertaking tasks, many of them can be taken without much effort. But there are some occasions when the repercussions of a choice can be severe, not only for ourselves but for others.

STONES

The verse in Ecclesiastes 3 about 'stones' being scattered and gathered has evoked much discussion. Experts fail to agree on exactly what it means. The Good News Bible uses the wording, 'the time for making love and the time for not making love' (v. 5, GNT). When compared to the New International Version it shows some diverging angles as to the interpretation of the original language! But whatever view is taken, there is an underlying sense that there are particular times when serious and far-reaching decisions, one way or the other, have to be made. They are going to have a significant impact both immediately and also in the future.

The problem is that such decisions may need to be made when those involved are inexperienced and have not previously been confronted with such demanding choices. When children are being raised it is most likely that adults, in various capacities, are charting the course ahead. But eventually young people have to make their own decisions in key areas such as exam subject options, relationships, peer group associations and family issues. Life can be really tough and the Teacher is right in drawing attention to the times when hard choices arise.

WARNING

An unpressurised environment in which to make decisions, with help from others, is therefore ideal. But whether on the threshold of wonderful opportunities, or on the brink of the inevitable – and everything in-between – such luxury is not guaranteed. Space and accurate information are also likely to be in short supply. So the Teacher's statement actually constitutes a warning. It's a case of telling us that times of scattering and gathering stones will come, and that the choices they represent cannot be avoided. Sometimes they may even require a split-second response. None of this is good news! So whatever the circumstances it raises the question: what preparations can be made to ensure that we are in the best possible place to either 'scatter' or 'gather'?

INVOLVING GOD

For those of us who are Christians there might seem an obvious starting point. This is that in having a relationship with God we are ready to involve Him in the decision process. However, this isn't always straightforward or clear-cut. On one occasion I met with a friend for what was initially a time of 'catching up'. But when he told me that he had applied for a change of job to a location 200 miles away I realised that this was not going to be a casual conversation! The repercussions of any decision could mean the uprooting of his home and family. This was why he asked my opinion on whether he should take up the offer of an interview that had resulted from his application. I simply felt that a step-by-step approach was needed. As he had been given the opportunity of an interview it seemed right to go through with it. The outcome should then be left to God. After chatting about the implications, I suggested that we pray... where we were sitting in a busy pub! While not the ideal environment, it was important that we recognised God's involvement in the situation and the decisions needing to be faced.

But involving God was something noticeably absent from the agenda of Joshua, the leader of the Israelites described in the Old

Testament. This failure probably comes as a reassurance to the rest of us who would not otherwise put ourselves in the same spiritual 'league' as him. His experience comes as a warning. Whether faced with the option to 'scatter' or 'gather' we have to make the conscious effort to focus on God. Perhaps, like us, Joshua was simply 'running on empty' at the time when the particular situation arose. He had just seen the miraculous power of God reduce the walls of mighty Jericho to rubble. The Promised Land now lay open before God's people. The emotional and spiritual toll of those past seven days had probably been substantial. Immediately ahead of them was the town of Ai. Spies had reported that only 'a few people live there'. But the relatively small force that Joshua then despatched was soundly beaten. Far worse than the fatalities that were sustained was the effect of this defeat on the Israelites. 'At this the hearts of the people melted in fear' (Joshua 7:4).

PERSPECTIVE

In military terms the action of Joshua was probably correct. But unfortunately none of our actions or decisions can be based on purely outward evidence. We are spiritual beings living in a material and spiritual world. Both systems involve principles being in operation. Joshua's plight had arisen because of not seeking God's perspective. With that defeat he had no option but to come to God. This was probably a case of 'better late than never'. God's response was to show him that defeat had arisen because of the flagrant disobedience of one man involved in the previous sacking of Jericho. Achan had stolen and hidden plunder from that city although God had directed that everything was to be destroyed. But God knew what this man had done, with the knock-on effect of bringing defeat upon the whole community. Sin is serious and can have far-reaching consequences. Joshua found this out the hard way. Dealing with Achan's sin meant severe action. Having identified him, there was a literal 'gathering' of stones. These were then thrown at him (Joshua 7:24–25; see also the Mosaic law in Leviticus 20:2, 27). This method of capital punishment may seem drastic to us but it underlined the need to deal with sin. Decisions cannot be made in isolation without involving God and taking into account the spiritual perspective.

CLOSENESS

The idea of 'gathering' stones brings a picture of another principle on which decision-making should be based. This points to the Old Testament practice of constructing altars and memorials. These were particularly striking reminders of wholly following God (Genesis 31:43–47; Joshua 22:26–27; 1 Kings 18:31–32). Being close to God, exemplified in this way, is important in exercising key choices. Such an action was again one which featured Joshua. In making the choice to obey God and lead the Israelites in crossing the River Jordan – a miracle comparable to the Red Sea parting – instructions were issued. These included representatives of each of the tribes taking a stone from the riverbed as it was traversed. The 12 stones were then set up as a marker on the west bank to remind future generations of God's miraculous intervention (Joshua 4:21–24).

RELATIONSHIP

However, being close to God is not simply a matter of adhering to instructions. If that were the case then, it might be conjectured, all we need to do is to receive heavenly emails and act on their content! There is clearly more that is involved. This moves us on to a final aspect of decision-making and links up with the Teacher's second part of the couplet: 'a time to embrace and a time to refrain'. The importance of relationship is underlined. There are times when we need to have very close relationships, and times when we need to separate. In this context it is helpful to see that Abraham, the great patriarch, was described as 'God's friend' (see 2 Chronicles 20:7), and that Moses was recorded as communicating with God 'as one speaks to a friend' (Exodus 33:11). Jesus underlined this relationship with His disciples: 'I no longer call you servants, because a servant does not know his master's business. Instead I have called you friends' (John 15:15).

There may be times when we are specifically challenged about this deep relationship with God. As Joshua's life was coming to a close he addressed the tribes of Israel. After giving an overview of God's work in the preceding generations, he confronted them with this issue:

> Now fear the LORD and serve him with all faithfulness. Throw away the gods your ancestors worshipped beyond the River Euphrates and in Egypt, and serve the LORD. But if serving the LORD seems undesirable to you, then chose for yourselves this day whom you will serve ... But as for me and my household, we will serve the LORD.
>
> (Joshua 24:14–15)

FOR REFLECTION

1. In what areas have you had to make big decisions? How hard was it to involve God at such times?

2. Why is it important to try and obtain more time and space in making significant choices rather than be pressured into giving snap decisions?

3. What is the value of making some form of physical reminder of times when we have chosen to follow God in a more committed way?

4. Making a verbal commitment to God can be a powerful means of declaring our decision to follow Him. What hymns and worship songs can you find to use in that respect?

15

STUFF – HOLDING ON OR LETTING GO?

... a time to search and a time to give up; a time to keep and a time to throw away ...
(Ecclesiastes 3:6)

'Stuff' dominates the thinking of most people. Many things can constitute 'stuff', such as money, possessions or housing. But you don't actually have to possess it to be fixated by it. The penniless and homeless refugee wandering around war-torn territory is likely to want it as much as the mega-rich oligarch living in a city penthouse. However, the former may want very different kind of stuff from the latter. Clean water, shelter, warm clothes and wholesome food would be uppermost in the minds of the destitute.

Sadly most of us take the commonplace stuff for granted. We simply don't appreciate much of what we possess or have around us. That's until something happens and we realise how vital something has been. Gratitude for the facilities and conveniences that we enjoy is often lacking.

POSSESSIONS AND PROPERTY

The Teacher, compiling this list of life events as inspired by God, now turns our attention to 'stuff'. The original wording of this verse in Ecclesiastes showed the immediate context as relating to material possessions or property. The message that is brought in that context is a disturbing one... especially as we put so much value and effort into acquiring and maintaining stuff. Different versions of the Bible present some stark facts on the subject:

> A time to get and a time to lose; a time to keep, and a time to cast away (KJV)

> A time to seek, and a time to lose; a time to keep, and a time to cast away (ESV)

> A time to gain, And a time to lose; A time to keep, And a time to throw away (NKJV)

As previously stated, this list of life events is not a series of options. The Teacher is telling us that these are all situations which, to a lesser or greater extent, we will all encounter. Such events may have to be faced more than once. So these verses can, in some circumstances, constitute a necessary warning. This is not necessary good news! Especially in terms of this verse (v. 6) where we are told that there are going to be times of having to 'lose', 'cast' or 'throw' away! Loss can be painful and emotionally disturbing. But there is also a powerful spiritual dimension to obtaining and losing possession.

EARNING A LIVING

This couplet starts with a positive perspective, as we may view it. There will be a time (or times) when we will 'gain' or 'get'. These will involve being in a mode whereby we will 'seek' or 'search'. One of the principles of life that God speaks about in the Bible is the importance of work and employment. This was a factor of life even before events described as 'the Fall'. It is stated: 'The Lord God took the man and put him in the Garden of Eden to work it and take care of it' (Genesis 2:15). Subsequent to the disobedience of Adam and Eve there was a pronouncement issued by God in respect of work: 'By the sweat of your brow you will eat your food' (Genesis 3:19). The apostle Paul updated the relevance of work when writing to other Christians: 'Make it your ambition to lead a quiet life; you should mind your own business and work with your own hands, just as we told you' (1 Thessalonians 4:11; see also 2 Thessalonians 3:11–12).

This points to the necessity of searching for appropriate and useful ways of earning an income enabling us to access the basics of life. There are, in the UK, a considerable number of opportunities, internet 'tools' and organisations (both governmental and private) available in this respect. However, the onus is largely on the client or customer to access these facilities, at least initially. The availability of free training courses, professional mentoring and advice, together with free internet access, all contribute to helping generate the needed momentum. But the 'time' to 'search' is an important underlying element.

Yet there can be negative experiences in the world of work. These may include redundancy, relocation, downsizing, health issues, reduced hours and retirement. Not only is the help and support of secular organisations needed but also the prayer and care of Christian friends. In the UK there have been a number of Christian organisations established to combine practical and spiritual support. One of these is PECAN (Peckham Evangelical Churches Action Network) in London. Over many years this group has facilitated employment preparation classes, one-to-one advice, ESOL classes and mental health recovery groups. Showing God's love in the community by this means underlines the fact that He cares about times when people are in need, including periods of unemployment.

DECLUTTERING

The adoption of a proactive stance is also necessary in times when we need to 'give up' or 'lose'. Terms such as 'downsizing' or 'decluttering' underline this conscious and deliberate decision to get rid of 'stuff'. This action may be purely pragmatic, arising from the need to move to a smaller property in a cheaper location in order to reduce expenses. There can also be altruistic reasons.

But there may also be times when we lose or give up certain stuff in circumstances outside of our control. This is not necessarily the result of theft or malicious activity. We have to face the fact that stuff wears out, becomes obsolete, irreparably breaks down, depreciates or is no longer fit for purpose. Replacement may not be viable. In that context Jesus brought this reminder: 'Do not store up for yourselves treasures on earth, where moths and vermin destroy, and where thieves break in and steal' (Matthew 6:19).

PREPARATION

What can we do in order to be ready for such times? The Teacher's warning doesn't include the preparation that we might need to take in order to 'soften the blow'. But other passages in the Bible show a frame of mind that we put in place. These include the following:

- Attitude of trusting dependence upon God
  – He will provide (Philippians 4:19)

- Acknowledging that we are only being
  loaned stuff – everything belongs to God
  in the first instance (1 Timothy 6:17)

- Always being grateful to God for what we
  have been loaned (Philippians 4:11–13)

- Accepting that stuff won't be around for ever (1 Peter 1:24)

- Aiming to build up spiritual 'treasure
  in heaven' (1 Timothy 6:17)

- Appreciating people more than
  possessions (Philippians 2:1–4)

KEEPING...

In the light of the temporary and distracting nature of stuff, we need to understand the importance of keeping a light hold on it, as distinct from 'it' having us in its hold. However there may be occasions when we specifically need to keep 'it'. A number of such 'times' are described in the Old Testament narrative. Naboth refused to sell his vineyard to Ahab, King of Israel, when the latter approached him for it, or to exchange it when offered a seemingly better one in its place. This decision cost Naboth his life – he was executed on a false charge instigated on account of the king's sulking reaction after being refused (1 Kings 21). Prior to this event one of King David's warriors, named Shammah, literally stood his ground in a field of lentils. He successfully defended it against a troop of enemy Philistine soldiers (2 Samuel 23:11–12). In each case the land that was being held (or kept) had spiritual significance. It was not the monetary value that was important, but what it represented. The Israelites viewed their land as specifically given to them by God, provided for them to possess and cultivate. This enabled them to generate a livelihood but also hold it, on trust, for future generations. It was therefore their responsibility to maintain it, as under God, within their family allocation.

We might struggle to identify what other 'stuff' might represent something of spiritual value such as land or property in the Old Testament. Perhaps the most obvious example would be the Bible itself, representing God's Word in written form. The preservation of Bibles, and their ongoing distribution throughout the ages, has been miraculous. The well-known Dutch lady, Corrie ten Boom, was desperate to keep hold of her Bible when transferred to a concentration camp in World War Two. She and her sister had been arrested by the Nazis for helping Jews avoid capture. Betrayed, they were designated for imprisonment. But despite being strip-searched they were able to successfully smuggle this forbidden Book into their terrible new surroundings. Spiritual life and hope was given to many of their fellow inmates as the Bible was subsequently read and studied (see her book, *The Hiding Place*, Hodder & Stoughton, 2004).

...AND THROWING AWAY

We need discernment from God as to what stuff we need to 'keep' at specific times. But, finally, we also need help in knowing when to 'throw' or 'cast' it away. Sometimes it might be quite obvious. When the apostle Paul was travelling to Rome, the ship in which he was travelling encountered a storm. This was so fierce that the cargo, together with non-essential equipment, was thrown overboard. Because of God's intervention everyone on board survived. But all the stuff, including the ship itself, was lost (see Acts 27).

Jesus' teaching about the beguiling distraction of money and possessions is well known. The Parable of the Sower includes the description of a thorn-infested environment. This was a 'picture'. 'The worries of this life, the deceitfulness of wealth and the desires for other things come in and choke the word, making it unfruitful' (Mark 4:19). Stuff can have a very negative spiritual 'pull'. But there is a positive angle. Passing on our wealth or possessions to others can prove a distinct blessing to the recipients, and therefore to ourselves.

There may be particular times when 'throwing away' may have a significant impact. Stuff, be it books, belongings, bank balances or bijou residences can have a spiritual dynamic about which we need to be aware. There will be times when we have to be prepared to deal with possessions as part of our relationship with God.

FOR REFLECTION

1. List some ways in which people can be helped to find work. How can individual churches assist people in periods of unemployment?

2. What's the value of having times of 'decluttering' even without financial pressures?

3. Apart from the Bible, what other possessions might come into the category of having spiritual value, making it necessary to retain them if possible?

4. Why is the account of the rich man's approach to Jesus important in our understanding about possessions (Mark 10:17–31)?

16

WORDS... AND THEIR IMPACT

... a time to tear and a time to mend, a time to be silent and a time to speak ...
(Ecclesiastes 3:7)

Research, such as findings released in 2013 by the University of Maryland, USA, has indicated that we probably speak, in the course of a normal day, around 20,000 words. This means that not only are we voicing a large number ourselves, but we are having to receive a sizeable volume from those around us. Not only are we listening to those in the immediate geographic vicinity, but also from the varied technical media sources that surround us. We live in an environment in which we are bombarded with words. They are an integral and intrusive aspect of our daily activities.

OTHER SOUNDS

However, through other scientific research we are also aware that audible sound is but a small spectrum of the 'noise' that rings around the created universe. Even the simple task of tuning an old radio demonstrates that there are unperceived conversations around us all the time. This is but a parable of the spiritual realm. The Bible records that there was 'rejoicing' and 'delighting' in the heavenly places when God spoke this world and humankind into being (Proverbs 8:27–31). Subsequently the angelic host could not restrain themselves when they later witnessed the birth of Jesus at Bethlehem. 'The Word became flesh' (John 1:14) to effect our salvation, and this warranted their verbal exclamation: 'Glory to God in the highest heaven, and on earth peace to those on whom his favour rests' (Luke 2:14). Heaven itself resounds with verbal acclamation of Jesus: 'Salvation belongs to our God, who sits on the throne, and to the Lamb' (Revelation 7:10). Such words of praise and adoration will endure for eternity.

God Himself is one who speaks words. He is described as using words to bring this world and creation into being: 'By the word of the Lord the heavens were made, their starry host by the breath of his mouth' (Psalm 33:6; see also Genesis 1:3, 'And God said …') When God became flesh, coming to this earth, words were an essential part of His ministry. It was through words that Jesus brought healing and release from demonic oppression, controlled nature, raised the dead, gave hope to the hopeless and spiritual enlightenment to those in darkness. Those words were not only spoken in power but also with an attitude of love and acceptance. This was beautifully summed up by the Gospel writer: 'All spoke well of him and were amazed at the gracious words that came from his lips' (Luke 4:22).

UNSEEN CONVERSATIONS
Now, as a consequence of these many voices, we can find ourselves being impacted with competing and contrary messages.

Many of these we simply do not recognise or realise to be significant. They are produced not only by people around us, both known and unknown, in the past as well as in the present, but also from within. Experiences, perhaps from a long time ago, reactions, reflections and imagination can all generate words that, as it were, we speak to ourselves, consciously or otherwise. The impact can be crucial and unrelenting.

CARE

So words are also incredibly powerful and need to be used with great care. They are not simply a physiological process by which our tongues cause airwaves to be disturbed, impacting our ear drums whose vibration is interpreted by our minds as communicating a message. There is much more involved. The apostle James summed up this unseen power:

> Likewise, the tongue is a small part of the body, but it makes great boasts. Consider what a great forest is set on fire by a small spark. The tongue also is a fire, a world of evil among the parts of the body. It corrupts the whole body, sets the whole course of one's life on fire, and is itself set on fire by hell ... It is a restless evil, full of deadly poison. With the tongue we praise our Lord and Father, and with it we curse human beings, who have been made in God's likeness. Out of the same mouth come praise and cursing. My brothers and sisters, this should not be.

> (James 3:5–10)

In the light of such devastating comments it's not surprising that the psalmist prayed: 'Set a guard over my mouth, Lord; keep watch over the door of my lips' (Psalm 141:3).

The Teacher in this Old Testament passage was inspired to include instruction about the words that we speak. So this verse in Ecclesiastes, underlining the awareness that there are times to be silent and times to speak, starts by referring to the power of words. As well as James, other New Testament writers wanted to point out the use to which they should be put. They wrote about their value in bringing discipline, admonition, prohibition and vital teaching. Words which brought 'mending' needed to be set alongside those which brought 'tearing'. The apostle Paul linked these two aspects when writing to Timothy, his protégé: 'Preach the word; be prepared in season and out of season; correct, rebuke and encourage – with great patience and careful instruction' (2 Timothy 4:2). Another church leader, Titus, was told by Paul to be very firm in what he said! 'Therefore rebuke them sharply ...' (Titus 1:13). The writer of the Proverbs pointed out that there is an appropriateness when talking: 'A person finds joy in giving an apt reply – and how good is a timely word!' (Proverbs 15:23). In these different forms of admonishment and encouragement, there can be a time of 'tearing' and a time of 'mending' in the spiritual lives of people.

SILENCE... AND NOT HOLDING BACK

Words are powerful not only when they are spoken, but also when they are absent. James wrote: 'Everyone should be quick to listen, slow to speak ...' (James 1:19). There may be times when this applies not only in respect of other people – holding back when provoked or emotionally stressed – but also in respect of our times with God. We are too quick to tell Him about our opinions, desires, actions and achievements. Times of quietness before God are spiritually humbling and yet enhancing. The psalmist learned this lesson: 'But I have calmed and quietened myself; I am like a weaned child with its mother; like a weaned child I am content' (Psalm 131:2).

Similarly there are encouragements for us not to hold back when it comes to approaching God. One of the most vivid aspects of teaching that Jesus brought in respect of this was prefaced: 'Then Jesus told his disciples a parable to show them that they should always pray and not give up ['not to faint', KJV; 'not lose heart', ESV] (Luke 18:1). This is linked with boldness in coming to God, described earlier in Luke:

> Then Jesus said to them, 'Suppose you have a friend, and you go to him at midnight and say, 'Friend, lend me three loaves of bread; a friend of mine on a journey has come to me, and I have no food to offer him.' And suppose the one inside answers, 'Don't bother me. The door is already locked, and my children and I are in bed. I can't get up and give you anything.' I tell you, even though he will not get up and give you the bread because of friendship, yet because of your shameless audacity he will surely get up and give you as much as you need.
>
> (Luke 11:5–8)

Whether approaching God with loads of words, or finding that words are simply inadequate, it's important that we come to Him. Human relationships can be deepened not only by verbal communication, but in sharing company with each other. There are times for both of these in respect of knowing God as our Heavenly Father. He fully understands 'where we are coming from', having 'compassion on those who fear him; for he knows how we are formed, he remembers that we are dust' (Psalm 103:13–14).

FOR REFLECTION

1. Even when words are needed to address negative issues in another person, what do you consider should be the approach or attitude behind what's said? How does this compare with what's taught in the New Testament letters (as above)?

2. What other different ways of bringing encouragement (a particular example of mending) can be used as well as verbal expression?

3. What is the value of having times of silence before God?

4. What is the value of speaking to God at times when we are alone?

17

LOVE AND HATE, WAR AND PEACE

... a time to love and a time to hate, a time for war and a time for

peace ...

(Ecclesiastes 3:8)

The different phases relating to time that the Teacher has highlighted in these verses from Ecclesiastes have not been easy to understand. They have also been challenging in their application. This final couplet is no more straightforward than any of its predecessors!

As with much of the content of this biblical book, we are required to stop and think in a way that we don't find easy. The approach towards life that the Jewish people held was not always the same as ours in the West and in the twenty-first century. This is evident from the teaching of Jesus where the use of hyperbole consistently featured. For instance Jesus spoke about a camel going 'through the eye of a needle', and a mountain being told: 'throw yourself into the sea' (Mark 10:25; 11:22). These deliberate exaggerations of speech (or writing) were being used for effect in order to underline or emphasise a point. In the cases just quoted they were in the context of a rich person entering the Kingdom of God, and showing the power of faith, respectively.

So one way of looking at these initial 'times' in which it was appropriate to 'love' and 'hate' is to view them in the light of other biblical references. The word for 'love' in this verse commonly appears in the Old Testament, used to describe the relationship between husband and wife, parent and child. So, for instance, God spoke to Abraham about his son Isaac, 'whom you love' (Genesis 22:1). Later, Isaac is described as marrying Rebekah: 'So she became his wife, and he loved her' (Genesis 24:67). But the word is also used to describe a relationship with God and an attitude towards Godly spiritual values. The psalmist often used the word to emphasise this need for closeness to God: 'Love the LORD, all his faithful people!' 'The LORD watches over all who love him' (Psalm 31:23; 145:20). But the psalmist also uses that other word, 'hate': 'Let those who love the LORD hate evil' (Psalm 97:10). He subsequently applies that word to people: 'I hate double-minded-people, but I love your law' (Psalm 119:113).

EMPHASIS

Clearly we are to love God and hate evil all the time. But particularly with regard to evil there may be times of specific focus. The psalmist added that he hated 'every wrong path', and 'falsehood' (Psalm 119:128, 163). God contributed His own list:

> haughty eyes,
> a lying tongue,
> hands that shed innocent blood,
> a heart that devises wicked schemes,
> feet that are quick to rush into evil,
> a false witness who pours out lies

and a person who stirs up conflict in the
community.

(Proverbs 6:16–19)

It needs to be noted that although there is a hatred of people this
is not conflicting with God's love for humankind. The attitude of
a person's heart and his or her rebellious stance against Him is
what He hates, as does the psalmist, being distinct from the
individual person.

The Teacher is therefore indicating that there are going to be
specific periods when our love and our hatred are to be particularly
energised. There will be times when our appreciation and
awareness of what God has done for us, and continues to do, will
cause an overflowing of deep love and gratitude. This is not to
say that, at other times, we are not in a relationship with Him or
love Him. It is simply that the reality of God's Father-heart is
more evident to us at some times in contrast to other occasions.

IN LINE WITH GOD

Similarly we may find that the horror of sin and waywardness is
more obvious to us than at other times. Clearly, on account of
our sin-infected environment and pedigree, this is an attitude that
needs to be developed. That process is otherwise termed
'sanctification'. It's likely to involve times of discipline, training
and hard work. These are ways of getting us in line with God's
attitude towards sin and evil. We are always to 'hate' all forms of
Godlessness, but the force of that attitude is likely to be more
apparent on occasions.

As the Teacher moves to speak about these last two linked
events, we are only too aware of the contrast. The existence of
war in all its forms, international and civil, together with

terrorism and acts of criminal violence are, tragically, ongoing and global in their effects. While we may, mercifully, be spared the direct impact of conflict, we cannot escape its consequences such as those of us in Europe seeing countless fleeing refugees entering the continent. They are not only from neighbouring countries, but from more distant locations such as Syria and Libya. In addition the threat of fundamentalist Islamic attacks means that security levels at airports, major termini and border posts are particularly and obviously heightened. Armed police are now a common sight, even in the streets of London.

DOES GOD APPROVE OF WAR?

Conflict has, sadly, been a constant feature of human history – an obvious and terrible outworking of people's failure to follow God and of their desire to put themselves in God's place. The vexed question arises: does God approve of war? Clearly this was not a feature of life as originally experienced in the Garden of Eden. But the wars subsequently suffered throughout ensuing history have been paralleled by spiritual battles in the heavenly realm. We have but a dim perception of these, with few biblical examples (see 2 Kings 6:15–17; Daniel 10:12–14; Luke 10:18).

However, it is evident that God has also executed judgement through very physical means. He allowed the enemies of Israel to oppress them in military and economic terms when they rejected Him and 'did their own thing'. But when His people repented, turned back to Him and asked for help, then He empowered a succession of Judges to wage war against those oppressors. The military action and achievements that followed were not on account of superior tactics or better armaments – quite the opposite! God brought victories through men and women such as Gideon, Deborah and Jephthah to show His power and to bring peace.

The history of the modern Western world does not show the same clear-cut involvement or direction of God in respect of engagement in war. However, the Teacher's explicit observation that there is a time for war indicates that, somehow in all of our experiences, this is not restricted to Old Testament accounts. Some secular historians have, for instance, argued that Great Britain could have avoided war in August 1914. Yet the belligerence of the Central Powers of Europe (Austria-Hungary, Germany) clearly demanded a robust response. The German Chancellor, Theobald von Bethmann-Hollweg, was amazed at Britain's declaration of war on account of what he described as 'a scrap of paper'. This document was Britain's agreement to come to the aid of a (basically) defenceless Belgium if her neutrality was threatened. It also has to be taken into account that, in pursuit of war, it was the Central Powers that first introduced unrestricted submarine warfare, poison gas, and the bombardment of civilians (in coastal towns from warships offshore, then by Zeppelin airships over London). The more widely known atrocities of the Axis Powers in World War Two added to those of the First.

PRINCE OF PEACE

Against this sombre background the writer of Ecclesiastes reminds us that there is also 'a time for peace'. That is God's aim, as indicated through the prophet:

> In the last days ...
> They will beat their swords into
>   ploughshares
>   and their spears into pruning hooks.

> Nation will not take up sword against
> nation,
> nor will they train for war any more.
>
> (Isaiah 2:2, 4)

Isaiah went on to prophesy of Jesus as the 'Prince of Peace' (9:6). His ministry on earth certainly demonstrated that in an environment of conflict, tension and brokenness, He was wanting and able to bring love, wholeness and *shalom* (peace). In the meantime such experiences may be spasmodic, just a 'taster' of what is to come. Perhaps that's why the Teacher was inspired to end with that word and the hope that it conveyed. God's 'shalom' is experienced personally as we spend time with Him!

FOR REFLECTION

1. What steps can we take to deepen our appreciable love for God?

2. In what ways can we make the 'pleasures of sin' less attractive?

3. What reaction should we have towards the seeming inevitability of wars and large-scale violence?

4. How can we experience more times of God's 'shalom' in our circumstances?

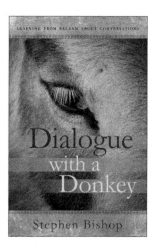

DIALOGUE WITH A DONKEY
Learning from Balaam about conversations
Stephen Bishop

A talking donkey and sword-wielding angel are the images most commonly associated with the Old Testament character of Balaam. Yet the significance and relevance of this account seem to be rarely considered.

"Dialogue with a Donkey" aims to open up this extraordinary story by looking at other conversations that were taking place… and which continue to do so. The compelling force of words to specifically direct, challenge, influence, affirm and develop people's lives are considered through Balaam's successive utterances. These pronouncements brought a divine perspective to the Israelites at that time. As this book advocates, we also need to hear what God is saying, breaking through all surrounding voices. It also underlines how Balaam's words reached a climax in pointing to Jesus who continues powerfully speaking into our darkness.

The stubborn donkey ends up being the means by which other people had God's life-giving word brought to them. We also need to hear such words. Are we listening?

ISBN 9781909824256
5.5 x 8.5" Paperback
Published by Zaccmedia

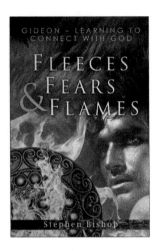

FLEECES, FEARS AND FLAMES
Gideon – Learning to connect with God
Stephen Bishop

Gideon is a well-known Bible character. His exploits in leading just three hundred men to defeat a huge invading army has inspired many people when faced with situations which are 'against-all-odds'. But how did it occur? Where was God in this scenario? How does this account relate to us?

'Fleeces, fears and flames' explores the Book of Judges in order to examine these ques-tions. Written in a down-to-earth manner, it looks at God connecting with Gideon despite his fears and fleece-laying doubts, then breaking through such frailty to release his power as seen in those flames. But it also shows that God is able to connect and work in our lives however daunting the challenges confronting us!

Suitable for individual reflection or group discussion, this material includes questions and a focus at the end of each main chapter to help connect the Biblical narrative in a personal way.

ISBN 9781909824492
5.5 x 8.5" Paperback
Published by Zaccmedia

FOCUSING BEYOND THE HORIZON
Samuel – Learning to see God's Perspective
Stephen Bishop

We relate to our surroundings by sight and sound. Together with our other senses we are able to interact with people and situations. But are these enough? Is more happening around us than we understand? Are we missing out on a further perspective?

This book, 'Focusing beyond the horizon,' looks at the Biblical character of Samuel in the Old Testament. Described as a prophet, or "seer", he saw more than the material world around him, being enabled to understand something of God's bigger picture.

Looking at the way in which God worked in Samuel's life, each bite-sized chapter in this material explores some of these factors and how we can also understand our world from God's viewpoint.

ISBN 9781909824737
5.5 x 8.5" Paperback
Published by Zaccmedia

FINDING A PLACE TO SETTLE

The Book of Ruth: Learning to find God-gifted identity
Stephen Bishop

Life is a journey. But this is not only in a geographical sense where some seem to travel much further than others! It also includes growing and shaping our character, sense of vocation and abilities. But where is it pointing us? The Bible describes a personal relationship with God as essential to life as He intended us to experience. However, such a 'faith journey' also means that we are finding out about ourselves.

The intriguing Book of Ruth in the Old Testament describes this woman's journey, physically, emotionally and spiritually. As well as discovering God working in her life 'behind the scenes' she also finds her God-gifted identity... an awareness that is relevant and important to us. These chapters explore some of the ways in which God brought this affirmation into her life. Questions are provided to apply the lessons of Ruth to ourselves, making this material suitable for both individual reflection and small-group discussion.

ISBN 9781911211242
5.5 x 8.5" Paperback
Published by Zaccmedia

Lightning Source UK Ltd.
Milton Keynes UK
UKOW06f1429200517
301636UK00001B/45/P